Are You There, Spirit?
It's Me, Travis

Are You There, Spirit? It's Me, Travis

LIFE LESSONS FROM THE OTHER SIDE

Travis Holp

S&G

Spiegel & Grau, New York
www.spiegelandgrau.com

Copyright © 2025 by Travis Holp

All rights reserved. No portion of this book may be reproduced, stored in a retrieval system, or transmitted in any form or by any means—electronic, mechanical, photocopy, recording, scanning, or other—except for brief quotations in critical reviews or articles, without the prior written permission of the publisher.

Interior design by Meighan Cavanaugh

Library of Congress Cataloging-in-Publication Data Available Upon Request

ISBN 978-1-954118-92-8 (hardcover)
ISBN 978-1-954118-93-5 (eBook)

Printed in the United States

First Edition
10 9 8 7 6 5 4 3 2 1

For Parker and Carter

Contents

Introduction
1

ONE
This Is Me
17

TWO
Hello
37

THREE
Trust Fall
55

FOUR
The Heart of the Matter
73

FIVE
Sunshine
87

SIX
Change
101

SEVEN
Socks
115

EIGHT
Butterflies
127

NINE
September
141

TEN
My Way
159

ELEVEN
Heaven Is a Place on Earth
177

Conclusion
201

Exercises 209
Acknowledgments 219
References 223
About the Author 225

Are You There, Spirit?
It's Me, Travis

Introduction

Hi, honey!

My name is Travis, and I'm a medium. If you don't believe in mediums, just consider me your gay uncle who knows a lot of shit. (Or you can think of me as your friend.) I want to start by saying thank you for being here on this journey with me. You and I are more deeply connected than you probably realize, and I am so grateful you chose to read my book.

Something magical and synchronistic (which, really, aren't those two things the same?) happened the week I met with Spiegel & Grau, the publishers that would agree to publish this book. My mom, who was moving at the time, found a large envelope in her filing cabinet. Inside was a manuscript for a book I had written at age eleven. Included with the manuscript was a letter to a publisher:

> *My name is Ty Holp. [Ty was my pen name for my writing career.] I was wondering if you would publish my book.*
>
> *PS—Please ignore the spelling errors. I did not notice them until it printed out. Then it was too late.*
>
> *—Ty Holp*

Even at that young age, I knew I wanted to be a writer, and it means so much to me that you are actually holding this book in your hands. It also means so much to my inner child, a sparkly eleven-year-old who wanted to bring joy to the world. This book is a collection of stories about love, connection, and the undeniable presence of Spirit. But more than that, it's a glimpse into my journey—not just as a medium but as a human navigating this wild, beautiful life.

A misunderstanding that exists about psychics, mediums, and spiritual teachers in general is that we must have life completely figured out. Honey, I do not want to burst your bubble, but we do not. I'm learning my lessons just like everyone else, and I don't get a free pass with Spirit. I'm just aware of the energy that exists beyond our physical senses and have learned and continue to learn how to work with this energy.

I want you to know right up front that I do not pretend to be an expert on grief, physical death, or the afterlife. The stories shared here are from client sessions, as well as from my own experiences.

INTRODUCTION

Some of the names and small details have been changed for the sake of client privacy, but the essence of each story is completely intact.

This book is being sent out into the world during one of the most transformational times in history. My hope is that it finds those who see themselves in these stories, recognize their loved ones in these readings, and feel the deep truth of the message that abundance is all around us, we are loved beyond measure, and there is always hope.

Throughout my life, I have faced self-doubt, criticism, trauma, and self-destruction, yet somehow, I found my way to healing—a path I can only describe as miraculous. And this book? It's filled with miracles. Every single one of them true.

My greatest wish is that you begin to notice the miracles unfolding in your own life. You don't need to believe in a specific god or follow any particular religion to receive them. The only thing required is the belief that miracles are possible—and the willingness to think you are worthy of receiving them. If you *know* it, even better. But simply *thinking* it is a beautiful place to start.

I share my own stories in these pages because I want you to see that, just like you, I am still learning, still growing, still on my own path of discovery. We are in this together.

In this book, I'll be using words like Spirit, energy, the Universe, God, Source, Heaven. Feel free to use whatever term resonates best with you to describe the energy that connects us all, or even to imagine your own word in place of mine. Words hold power, and so does the energy we put behind them; in fact, the energy behind them is even more potent.

My journey with Spirit has taught me something incredibly important—the foundation of every story in this book: We are more than our physical bodies. We are energy, frequencies. Just as color or sound vibrates at a specific frequency, so do our souls. That energy is limitless, transcending all we might understand about who we truly are. We enter our bodies as energy, we live as energy, and we leave as energy. Our bodies are mere vehicles for this experience; they don't define who we are. We are so much more.

My intention in writing this book is to gently remind you—as I am continually reminded—that your spirit is eternal and boundless. We indeed continue beyond this physical life, and we remain deeply connected to those who are no longer in physical form. You don't have to believe in the work I do, but I hope this book helps you believe in yourself.

We do not die. Our loved ones are not *dead*—they simply exist in a different frequency. They are still with us, guiding us, offering their love and support as we navigate this incredible journey in our human bodies. It is my belief that as souls—as pure energy—we have the ability to connect with our departed loved ones anytime we choose.

I also believe that anyone has the potential to do what I do. Now, when I say that, I mean it in the same way that everyone can sing. Technically, yes, we all have voices, but not everyone is meant to run off and make a career of it. Still, you don't *need* a medium to connect with your loved ones. A medium simply acts as a bridge between the seen and unseen worlds. We are like radios, gently tuning our frequencies to match the vibrations of those who have crossed over, receiving and broadcasting their messages to this world.

INTRODUCTION

Spirit communicates with me in multiple ways—through seeing, hearing, and feeling. When I *see*, Spirit shows me images—flashes of symbols or signs, like a set of spiritual flash cards I've developed with my team of Spirit Guides over time. For example, when I see rings that can mean someone is getting married, or balloons can signal that it's someone's birthday. A bottle of beer can mean someone had a drinking problem, and a hand holding an apple can mean that someone was or is a teacher. When I *hear*, it's not a voice in the way you'd hear a person speaking beside you—it's more like an energetic frequency, a buzzing that enters my awareness, and my brain translates it into words or messages. And then, there's *feeling*.

Feeling is my favorite. Yes, I'll feel how a person passed, but more important, I'll feel how they *loved*—how they cherished the person I'm reading for. I'll feel their joy, their excitement, their pride. I'll also feel their regrets or apologies, if there are any. To be able to experience all of this and communicate it is a privilege, a sacred gift that I hold with deep reverence.

As you move through the journey of this book, you'll begin to notice something intricately woven throughout its pages: *synchronicity*. It's one of the many ways our loved ones, Spirit Guides, and angels reach out to us. What we often brush off as mere coincidence is, more often than not, a perfectly timed message. I don't believe in coincidences. This vast, intricate, and deeply connected Universe is always listening, always responding. And that includes our loved ones, gently reminding us that they are near.

Synchronicity shows up in countless ways. Maybe you glance at the clock at *exactly* 11:11. Maybe you casually mention wanting to pick up a new hobby, and the very next day, you stumble upon a flyer for a class on that exact activity at your favorite coffee shop. Maybe you think about calling someone, only for your phone to ring with *their* name lighting up the screen before you even touch it.

These signs, symbols, and synchronicities guide us, whisper to us, remind us. You'll see them reflected in each chapter. I like to think of them as little winks from the Universe—loving nudges to remind us that we are never alone, that we are divinely supported, and that we are always, *always*, exactly where we're meant to be.

Coming Out

"When did you know you were a medium?" It's a question I get asked all the time. And my answer is always the same: *Always. I just didn't know that's what it was called.* Then comes the next question: "When did you know you were gay?" And, funnily enough, my answer doesn't change. *Always.*

I just didn't realize that the core of who I was—both as a medium and as a gay man—wasn't something that everyone experienced. I grew up in a small town outside of Dayton, Ohio, and let's just say we didn't exactly have a lot of *out-and-practicing* psychic mediums running around. The only ones I knew of were on TV—John Edward and Sylvia Browne. I didn't see a whole lot of openly gay people, either. The ones I *did* see? Also on TV. Obviously, both existed, but in my world, neither was visible to me. I'm sure the same can be said for others who were connected

INTRODUCTION

to spirituality—it wasn't something people talked about, let alone embraced.

The town I grew up in was predominantly Christian, white, and deeply heteronormative. I couldn't wait to see what else existed beyond it. Not because I *hated* it, but because I knew, deep down, that staying there meant hiding—forever. I thought coming out would be my great liberation. That once I finally said, "I'm gay," I'd be free. I was aware that my very conservative parents had fears about having a gay son. I wasn't about to casually throw in, "Oh, and by the way, I also talk to dead people." I'm pretty sure that would have sent them straight into exorcism mode. (Mostly a joke. But also . . . not.) So I kept my connection with Spirit to myself.

My earliest memory of Spirit communication was with my dad's mom—my granny.

H-E-L-L-O.

The planchette of the Ouija board moved my fingers from one letter to the next. "Hello! Granny! Granny! It said hello!" I squealed, running straight into my grandmother's arms. She wrapped her arms around me and kissed the top of my head, as the smell of her Estée Lauder Youth-Dew perfume, with its warm, intense amber and floral fragrance, filled my nose. I was six years old, and I spent my days with her while my parents worked at the restaurant they owned. She was one of my favorite people. Time with her was my favorite—dancing, singing, spending time with my cousins, and playing with the Ouija board she kept in her house.

"It did?!" she asked, settling onto the couch as she watched me play in what we called the Pink Room: Everything was pink—carpet, couches, curtains. Even now, if I close my eyes, I can still smell that room, its unique scent a mixture of floral perfume, warm fabric, and something distinctly Granny. I can feel the plush carpet under my feet, see the organ my granny used to play and the cabinets filled with delicate figurines and bells I loved to ring. The genie-lamp-shaped trinkets she had fascinated me. I'd rub them, pretending that a mystical being would emerge in a swirl of smoke. But the Pink Room wasn't just a place for games and dancing around to Britney Spears. (Yes, I choreographed dances for me and my cousins.) It was also where my granny kept her Ouija board.

"What else do you think it has to say?" she asked, sitting down on the floor beside me, placing her hands on the planchette next to mine. If you aren't familiar with a Ouija board, some believe it's a tool (one of many) for communicating with the Spirit world, while others dismiss it as nothing more than a parlor game.

As we sat together, a familiar sensation began to build. The energy of Spirit grew louder in my mind. When I was a child, whenever I sensed Spirit, my ears would ring, like someone was turning up the volume on a conversation I wasn't yet able to understand. I would also feel nervous or anxious. Sitting with the board amplified the effect. At the time, I didn't realize that this was something special within me. All I knew was that it felt like magic, and I didn't want it to stop. A thought bubbled up inside me, one I had never dared to voice. Something about being in this moment, with my granny beside me, made me feel safe enough to share with her. It was something that not even my parents knew.

INTRODUCTION

"Granny, can I tell you something?" My voice was barely above a whisper, my wide eyes searching hers for approval.

"Of course," she said, her expression soft and patient.

I hesitated, then admitted, "Sometimes I hear people who aren't there. And when we play this game, their voices get even louder. And sometimes . . . I feel like I'm not alone, even when no one else is in the room. And sometimes I'm afraid of the dark."

She didn't flinch. She didn't dismiss me. Instead, she stood up and motioned for me to sit with her on the couch. She wrapped her arms around me and kissed the top of my head. What she said next I would never forget.

"I know, Travis. You're very special. And I want you to always remember that I love you." She was the first person to know about my ability. And, perhaps, the first to sense something else about me, something I wouldn't fully understand until later. She also made me feel deeply loved.

We returned to the Ouija board, my curiosity at an all-time high. I was communicating with an unseen world, and I couldn't wait to keep going. More messages appeared: *Hello. I'm here. Love.* I was beaming with satisfaction, not just at the board's movement, but at the fact that I had finally shared my secret with someone. Instead of fear, I was met with understanding. It was as if my world had cracked open just a little bit wider. At that moment, I felt seen in a way I never had before. As we continued playing, I noticed something else: My granny wasn't afraid. She didn't recoil from the messages or dismiss them. She leaned into the experience with the same playful curiosity that she brought to everything in life.

That was Granny—open, loving, and full of wonder. I wanted to be just like her.

Later, when I told my parents about my experience with the Ouija board, my excitement quickly faded. I'd expected them to share in my amazement, to be just as intrigued as Granny was. But their reaction was far from warm. They dismissed any ideas that we had communicated with the other side. To them, the Ouija board was just a silly game. But my belief in what had happened, my certainty that I had connected with something beyond this reality, was steadfast.

As I continued to grow, I became fascinated with witches, magic, tarot, anything having to do with unseen energy. I felt so deeply drawn to that world, but when I told my family about my desire to continue to connect with the Spirit world, I was met with resistance and fear. I can still remember the shift in my parents' faces when I told them, the way their expressions became serious and their bodies stiffened. It was the first time I had ever felt shame about my connection to Spirit. Before that moment, it had felt like a gift, a special secret between me and the Universe. Suddenly, however, it was something to fear. Something to hide.

That was the first time I learned to silence a part of myself.

Granny crossed over suddenly at the age of sixty-six, right before I started to come out to my family. When she told me she knew I was special, I knew she didn't just mean because I could sense things that weren't in the physical world. She knew who I truly was. Even though we never had those final moments, we have had many connections since her departure from this physical world. I was brave enough to be who I was around her because of

INTRODUCTION

her ability to show love without judgment, but that wasn't the case with the other adults in my life. I would need to hide many things about myself, not just the fact that I talk to Spirit.

There are so many people with stories like mine. Over the years, I've given thousands of readings to people all over the world, and I've lost count of how many times someone has told me they were sensitive to energy as a child—only for it to either *quiet down* as they got older or shut off completely.

As children, we are wide open to the energy around us. We exist in a natural state of wonder, deeply connected to our creativity and imagination—both of which are direct channels to Source, Spirit, God, whatever name resonates with you. When we are in tune with our creativity, we allow that universal life force energy to flow through us, bringing joy, healing, abundance, and vitality. That same energy is also the essence of our loved ones in Spirit.

But as we grow, life teaches us to shut that part of ourselves down. We're encouraged to seek validation, security, and answers *outside* of ourselves rather than trusting the infinite source of wisdom *within*. Now, I'm not here to knock the material world. In fact, I believe living in it is both a blessing and a gift. But somewhere along the way, we forgot something important: that there is an energy that connects us all. And it's not *out there*—it's *within us*.

If you are thinking you don't have that connection to Spirit within you, I have news for you . . . You do. We all do. It's wired into us. For some it's like playing an instrument. One person might be able to play a piano flawlessly after only a few lessons, while another might take a few years of practice before they can play simple pieces. There is no race when it comes to connecting to your intuition or your loved ones who have departed. With our connection to Spirit, what matters most is consistency and trust. As an eternal being you are enterally growing and expanding. I joke with my clients that they shouldn't sweat what they feel they missed in this life because there is always next time. While there's humor in that, I also believe the core of that sentiment to be true.

A Moment to Surrender

I never set out to be a medium. In fact, I had a rewarding and successful seventeen-year career in the beauty industry. Then, one summer morning in 2020, I woke up on my living room floor after a three-day vodka bender. There's no pretty way to say this: I had a problem and was on a path to full destruction. I would drink and drink, justifying this behavior for over a decade. But my problem wasn't alcohol. Alcohol was something I had been using for fourteen years to numb what I was feeling. Numbing the loneliness, the shame, the guilt, the grief, even the sensing of others' psychic energy and the feelings I would receive when someone's loved one would try to communicate with me. I wanted to numb it all. Sometimes, I would drink so much that I would hope not to wake up the next day. And on that particular day, the collective energy of twenty years' worth of trauma and suffering had reached a tipping point.

My use of alcohol and occasional recreational drugs, as well as the anxiety and depression I had lived with for years, was deeply

INTRODUCTION

linked to my not allowing myself to be who I was. I was still hiding parts of myself away, and those parts of me had become wounded and damaged over time. I had a problem accessing my pain to be present with it and to hear what it was trying to tell me. I had abandoned myself repeatedly, only to be left so disconnected from myself that I didn't know who I was.

Then, the voice came.

Travis, if you keep drinking like this, you are going to die.

It came out of nowhere, but I knew it was real. I knew I was hearing something greater than myself.

"Then what on earth do you want me to do?" I finally said.

Meditate.

I had never meditated before, but I sensed that meditation was exactly what I needed. I pulled myself off the floor, sat upright, closed my eyes, and began to breathe—and quickly realized that I had no idea what I was supposed to be doing. But it didn't matter. I was ready to quit suffering, and this was my way out. My emotional pain had spread through my body and mind, like a poison. I had never before felt the venom of the suffering I was carrying, and I was ready to heal from it. This was the first time I acknowledged that I couldn't keep hiding. Then, I heard the voice again . . .

Hello. I'm here. Love.

I made a decision that day. I decided to stop drinking and to stop hiding. I couldn't promise that I wouldn't hide again, but I *could* promise to take brave steps forward. To do whatever it took to fill the emptiness with my own love and compassion instead of with substances. I didn't know what the path to healing was, but I knew that I was walking the path of suffering. And I knew that where I was, numbing was no longer working. I also knew that I had a purpose much bigger than myself and that in order for me to live into that greater vision for my life, I needed to get the hell out of my own way.

Once I decided to begin diving into the old wounds that had been causing me to numb myself to the world around and within me, things got interesting. My dreams became even more intense, and I could begin to feel, hear, and see energy around me just as I had when I was a child. It was as if someone had turned up the volume knob on my psychic senses. For a little while I thought that maybe, perhaps, I was losing my mind. I had a secret tarot deck that I used to give friends readings back when I drank—please do not drink and divinate!—and I pulled a few cards for myself, but of course that wasn't satisfying enough. I decided I would need expert advice.

At the time, I was in the process of moving from Phoenix, where I had been living for a brief time, to Washington state. I found a psychic and tried to book an appointment with her, but her schedule was full. Then, the night before my move, she called to say that she had a last-minute opening, and naturally I took this as a big sign from the Universe that I needed to meet with her.

The first thing Teri said to me was: "Honey, you're a medium." The moment she said those words, I felt my whole body relax. It was the feeling of being seen and understood. Like I was holding on to a secret, and it was now okay to be different.

I had never consulted a psychic medium before, and I was amazed when she described everything I had ever experienced growing up, from being deeply sensitive to hearing Spirit when

INTRODUCTION

I was younger to using alcohol to tune it out and numb my loneliness. It was as if she had a full transcript of my life leading up to the moment when I was seated in front of her. I felt seen and validated but also uneasy because I had no idea what any of this could mean. She mentioned specific memories I had of both my grandmothers and told me they were watching over me but that I was still healing from the passing of one of them.

"You know, Travis, one day you will do what I'm doing. You are meant to help people."

"No way," I said. I had a stable career in the beauty industry and couldn't see myself anywhere else.

The Universe, however, knew different. It would just take some time and some surrender on my part. Looking back now, I can see perfectly how all the events in my life led to the unfolding of where I am now, but I couldn't see it then. And I suppose that's the whole point: We often have no idea where we are headed, but when we look back, we can see the path to where we ended up with perfect clarity. I left the reading feeling validated but still unsure how to let myself tap into the deeper awareness that I knew was there but was too afraid to connect with. What followed was more hiding and more avoiding the deeper truth within myself.

By the time I met with a second psychic, it was September 2020. I had just left my career in beauty, and at this point I was a few months sober. Once again, this second psychic described in perfect detail everything I had gone through growing up and what I was currently experiencing, down to the ear ringing. (I had recently had my ears checked and everything was "normal.") Naturally, the second time someone shared with me that I had psychic abilities, I paid more attention. The psychic suggested I read a few books on mediumship, maybe find a class on connecting to Spirit, and that's exactly what I did. I began to study, and what I realized was that I wasn't necessarily learning something new but rather remembering something that was already deep within me.

I began giving readings on a whim. Like most big turning points in my life, showing up to give tarot readings on TikTok didn't feel like a massive leap, it just felt natural. And then live tarot readings on TikTok became private tarot readings with actual clients. Eventually I would realize that the cards were just helping me channel and that Spirit was leading me the entire time.

This book, dear reader, is about my journey of leaning into Spirit and trusting the divine wisdom that is available to all of us—not just to mediums. Thank you for being here, for reading these stories, and for keeping your heart open to the possibility that anything is possible because you are an unlimited being.

I love you, and I'm incredibly proud of you.

—Travis

ONE

This Is Me

The first time I ever gave someone a message from Spirit was the first time I truly felt whole. I was in the middle of a reading for someone who had found me through TikTok. We were on the phone when I kept hearing the name Buck over and over again. It was relentless, like a drumbeat repeating in my mind.

Finally, I asked, "How do you understand the name Buck? Who is Buck to you?"

The woman went quiet for a moment, and then she said, "Buck was my uncle. He passed away just two weeks ago."

I was stunned. I had only been reading tarot, and connecting to Spirit for other people wasn't something I had done regularly. Most of my readings were psychic readings, which means I'm connecting to the energy of those here in physical bodies. This connection to Buck, who was departed, was something I hadn't planned on.

I took a deep breath, and suddenly, Buck showed me an image of small stones being placed around a grave. The vision was clear, almost tangible.

"Do you understand what these small stones are?" I asked.

She gasped. "My children placed small stones around where we buried him the other day. We do not have the headstone yet, but they wanted him to know we did not forget him."

All I heard next was a simple yet deeply heartfelt *thank you*.

I shared that message with her, and in that moment, something *shifted*. The connection was brief, but it was *real*. It wasn't something I could rationalize away or chalk up to coincidence. It was something *undeniable*.

For the first time in my life, I felt complete. It was as if the entire Universe had aligned perfectly, every experience leading me to that precise moment. I wasn't searching, I wasn't questioning—I *knew*. I was exactly where I was meant to be.

And with that knowing came a certainty so deep, so absolute, that it anchored itself in my soul: *I never want to lose this feeling*. That feeling of connection. Of purpose. Of being part of something so much greater than myself. It was unlike anything I had ever known before. Not just because of what I had experienced, but because, for the first time in my life, I felt like *me*. Not a version of myself I had carefully shaped for the world. Not a version that had been filtered through fear, doubt, or expectation. Just *me*. And I needed to know more. I needed to understand what had happened, why it had happened, and how I could step further into it.

Because something inside me had awakened. And there was no going back.

Over the next few months, I threw myself into learning. I devoured every mediumship book I could get my hands on, desperate to understand how this connection worked. I joined Spirit circles, sitting with others who shared my curiosity, exchanging messages from the other side and witnessing moments of profound validation. I meditated daily, setting a clear intention to bridge the gap between this world and the next. I wasn't just dipping my toes in—I was fully immersed, determined to unlock whatever door had been opened inside me.

As a Virgo, I've always been drawn to rules, structure, and systems. I like knowing *how* things work, what steps to follow, what method produces the best results. So I approached mediumship the same way. I wanted a guidebook, a checklist, a formula that would tell me: *This is how you talk to Spirit. This is how you receive messages. This is what it should look like.*

But Spirit doesn't work like that.

There is no set structure, no rule book, no perfect method. Connecting with Spirit isn't about control—it's about surrender. It's about getting quiet, opening up, and trusting in something beyond what the logical mind can grasp.

That was hard for me.

At first, I second-guessed everything. Was that my imagination or a real message? Was I making this up? Was I *doing it right*? But as I gained experience—through practice, through readings, through moments of undeniable proof—I learned something even more valuable than technique:

I learned to trust myself.

I learned that mistakes were part of the process. That messages don't always come in clear, perfect sentences, but rather through symbols, sensations, and flashes of knowing. I learned that I didn't need to control every aspect of it—because the more I tried to control, the harder it was to receive.

More than anything, I allowed myself to be *who I truly was*.

And that was something I had struggled with my entire life. But in this work—through the messiness, the uncertainty, the moments of magic—I started to find my way.

A Doctor, a Therapist, and a Youth Minister

When I first came out, my mom had a tough time accepting that her son was gay. And to be fair, I told her I *thought* I was gay. Somehow, I convinced myself that softening the statement—leaving room for doubt—might also soften the impact. Spoiler alert: It didn't. Instead, my mom took my attempt to mitigate her pain as an opportunity to "help" me, to *fix* me. She took me to three different people, hoping they'd tell me that being gay was a choice. And I know, I *know*, this sounds like the setup to a joke, but this actually happened: She took me to our family doctor, our family therapist, and for the grand finale, a local youth minister.

She was looking for validation; she was hoping that someone in a position of authority would tell me I was wrong about myself. But instead—without realizing it—she led me straight to the first adults in my life who would affirm *me*.

Now, let me preface this by saying that my mother is a wonderful mother. I know she loved me then, just as she loves me now. But at the time, she was consumed by fear. Fear of what my life would look like. Fear of what people would say. Fear that my being gay meant something about her as a mother. And of course, I had my own healing to do—because regardless of her intent, her actions had left a mark. Coming out to her didn't feel like a moment of liberation. It felt like a battle I had to fight just to be myself.

STOP #1: The Family Doctor

We went to my doctor under the guise of a routine checkup, but even as I sat alone in the cold exam room, I knew something was off. I could hear my mom and the doctor talking just outside the door—loudly. Loud enough that I caught pieces of the conversation, and loud enough that I heard the doctor raise her voice at my mother.

When the doctor finally walked into the exam room, she sat down in front of me, looked me in the eyes, and said, "Travis, being gay is not a choice. Your mother wants me to tell you that it is, but I just don't believe that. Please let me know if I can help you in any way."

The doctor had tears in her eyes. And I remember thinking, *Why are you crying? You're not the one being told you need to be fixed.* But looking back, I realize that the moment was significant. It was the first time an adult looked at me with empathy regarding my sexuality. Growing up, I had always been told that being gay was wrong. There was never space for conversation, never an opportunity to be seen or understood. So when my doctor looked at me with sadness but also care, I didn't know what to do with it.

STOP #2: The Family Therapist

Next up was our family therapist. I liked him—he was kind and thoughtful. I had been seeing him for about a year to work through my parents' divorce, and I trusted him. Once again, my mother had a private conversation with him before I entered his office. And once again, when I sat down, I heard the same thing: "Your mom wants me to tell you that you're choosing to be gay. But I can't tell you that because I don't believe that's true."

He was adamant about it. There was no hesitation, no waffling to spare her feelings. He didn't just refuse to lie—he made sure I knew that he knew the truth. Then he asked me something no adult had ever asked me before. "Do you need anything?"

And of course, I did what I always did—I smiled. I told him I was fine. That I didn't need anything at all.

But the truth?

I desperately needed to be myself, without constriction. Without hiding. Without feeling as if I had to make myself smaller to fit into something I was never meant to be.

Here's the thing: I have *always* been what some people would call effeminate. My voice is naturally higher. I love sparkly pink things. There has always been a softness in how I speak, in how I move through the world.

For a long time, I hated that about myself.

I tried to act more masculine, but it never felt right. It was like putting on a costume that didn't fit. And let me tell you, I wasn't very good at it. Watching me attempt to deepen my voice and stiffen my posture was like watching a dog trying to walk on its hind legs—awkward, unnatural, almost comical.

Growing up, I loathed my voice. The kids at school teased me relentlessly for it. But isn't it funny how life works? The very thing I was bullied for—the thing I wanted to change *more than anything*—ended up being my greatest gift. Because with my voice, I get to help others. I get to speak messages from Spirit, to offer comfort, to connect.

What once felt like a curse became my *superpower*.

FINAL STOP: The Youth Minister

Our last stop on this being-gay-is-a-choice tour was a Christian youth minister.

My family wasn't particularly religious. We weren't consistent churchgoers. We'd go for a few weeks, and then life would happen and we'd stop. But even though we weren't in church every Sunday, my parents still used the Bible to condemn things they didn't understand. That was very common in Ohio—and I know it's common in a lot of places.

Honestly? I think that's the lazy route. Condemning something with a book you don't even fully understand, as if my existence was something to apologize and repent for? Little did I know, this visit with the minister would change the way I viewed my life here on Earth.

I tell this story not to villainize my mother but to paint an honest picture of how deeply ingrained fear and misunderstanding can be. My mom loves me. I have never questioned her love for me. But at that time in her life, she was operating from fear, from societal conditioning, from a belief system that told her that something was wrong with me when there was never anything wrong to begin with.

And the beautiful thing? Since then, my parents have grown. They have expanded. They have evolved. They have learned that love is bigger than the constraints of old beliefs. And for that, I am eternally grateful.

Because love—*real* love—isn't about control. It's not about trying to change someone into something more comfortable for *you*. Love is expansive. Love allows. Love makes room.

And the greatest thing I ever did for myself was make room for *me*.

From the moment the youth minister greeted me in his office, I could tell he was trying to make me feel comfortable in a space that could easily cause unease for someone like me. He was cheerful and overly friendly. He dressed like he had just come from a Christian rock concert—band T-shirt, baggy jeans, the whole look. He spoke to me as if we were the same age, even though he was well into his forties and I was fourteen.

What he didn't know was that he was about to give me advice that would change the course of my life forever. Advice that is the reason you're reading this book right now.

We started off with light conversation—he asked how my day was going, what subjects I liked in school, what I wanted to do after high school. And for a moment, I thought, *Maybe this isn't going to be so bad. Maybe he's actually a nice guy.*

Then he hit me with it.

"So your mom tells me that you think you might be gay."

I didn't *think* I was gay. I *knew* I was gay. In fact, I wanted to stand on the nearest rooftop and scream it: "I'm gay! I'm gay! I sparkle! I shine! I radiate rainbows! *I am gay!*" Instead, I looked him in the eye and simply said, "Yeah, I do think I'm gay."

He nodded, leaned in a little, and said, "Well, Travis, I'm going to keep it real with you, my friend. You know that the Bible says that's a sin and that your soul will spend the rest of eternity in hell."

All I could think in that moment was: *Isn't this hell?*

Having to hide who I was. Feeling I had to shrink myself to make other people comfortable. Watching the people I loved struggle to love me back fully because they were afraid.

Then, his tone shifted. "Travis, you are not your body or your human self. You are a soul. Do you know what that means?" He leaned forward as if he was about to reveal some deep, ancient secret.

I hesitated. "I mean . . . I think so?"

I had heard the word *soul* before, mostly in church when my family actually went. My fourteen-year-old brain couldn't quite wrap itself around the concept, but somehow, energetically, I understood exactly what he was saying.

"Your soul comes from God," he continued, "and therefore, you are an extension of God."

I nodded. "Okay, I'm following." Even though, logically, I was still lost, something deep inside me was listening.

"Do you know what eternity is?" he asked.

"It sounds like forever," I said with a little smile, knowing full well what eternity meant.

"Your soul exists for all of eternity."

And the second he said it, I knew it was true. I felt the truth of his statement in every part of my being.

He kept going. "Here's the deal, T." (T? All right.) "Your soul is here for all of eternity, and that's just the way it is. Think of eternity like a never-ending cable. But your time here in this human body?" He pinched his fingers together. "It's a razor-thin slice of that never-ending cable. That's all you get here in this life."

I stared at him, not sure where he was going with this.

"So, you've got to make a decision," he continued. "How will you spend that tiny little slice? The slice that's going to determine what happens to you for the rest of eternity. How are you going to fill that razor-thin slice?"

And while I didn't fully understand everything he was saying, in that moment, I understood the core of it.

Not only did I understand it—I *knew* it.

See, belief is one thing. Belief is just a thought we've had over and over again. And belief leaves room for doubt. But *knowing*?

Knowing is *absolute*.

In that moment, the youth minister gave me the best gift I had ever been given in my life. He made me *aware*—aware that my time in this physical body is limited. And I wasn't about to waste a single second of it being something I wasn't.

I looked him directly in the eye and said, "Thank you so much. You have given me exactly what I needed today to know how to live my life."

His face lit up. "I'm so glad I could help."

Me, too, I thought.

I stood up, walked out of that room, and knew—*without a shadow of a doubt*—that my life had just changed forever.

Coming Out of the Broom Closet

Much like I did with the Ouija board when I was younger, I sat down to tell my mother I was gay because I had learned a beautiful truth that I had to share with her. I was no longer confused, no longer questioning. I wasn't going to pretend anymore or soften my words with "I *think*" just to make them easier for her to hear. I *knew* I was gay.

And while we were at it, why not throw in that I could also connect with spirits who were no longer in the physical world?

When I told her, her fear took over.

She immediately started telling me I was going to hell, that no one would love me if I was gay, and that if I was truly gay, I couldn't live in her house.

So I did what I had learned to do from a young age.

I hid.

I told my mom I was just confused, that it was probably a phase, that it would pass. I swallowed the truth of who I was—again.

And so, once more, I learned to pretend.

I wouldn't officially come out to her again for a few more years. In the meantime, I got really good at hiding. Not just at hiding my flamboyance or my love for pink sparkly things. Not just hiding my ability to connect with Spirit.

I hid my *heart*.

I hid the way I love. The way I care. The way I offer kindness, empathy, and deep understanding to others. Because somewhere along the way, I had learned that those parts of me—the *soft* parts—could get me rejected.

So I replaced them. With frustration. With anger. With sadness.

When we suppress who we truly are, a tension arises within us—something that festers, builds, and grows into resentment. And resentment, over time, becomes anger. And if that anger has nowhere to go? It sinks into sadness. It takes root. It turns into depression, into anxiety, into a heaviness we carry without realizing how much of it was *never ours to hold in the first place*.

At least, that was my experience. By the time I was ready to come out to my family and friends *again*—this time as a medium—I expected the same reaction I had received when I came out as gay. But that couldn't have been further from the truth.

I still remember the moment vividly. I was standing in the middle of Target, of all places. By that point, my TikTok account had taken off, and I had several hundred thousand followers. I knew I needed to tell my mom before she inevitably found out from someone else.

So right there in the middle of the store, during a moment of bravery and a desire for her to hear it from me and not someone else, I called her. The words "Mom, I'm a psychic medium, and I help people" fell right out of my mouth. I'm not sure I even said hello.

To be honest, I don't think she fully understood what I was telling her, but to my surprise and delight she was incredibly supportive. Then she told me something that made my whole face light up:

"Your nanan [her mother] used to see psychics all the time. She really believed in all that stuff! She loved having her tarot cards read and getting psychic readings."

Learning about my nanan and her fascination with psychics brought an unexpected feeling of joy. Not only was my granny (Dad's mom) connected to unseen energy, my nanan had an appreciation and belief in it, too. My mother's acceptance, and learning about my nanan's interest in the esoteric, allowed me to step into my own authenticity.

Authenticity

The journey to authenticity is about understanding who we are on a deeper level. It's about peeling back the layers of fear, shame, and conditioning that tell us we can't be ourselves. One of my first mentors said to me, "Travis, the best advice I can give you is this: Get the hell out of your own way."

At the time, I had no idea what they meant.

But looking back now, I know exactly what they were trying to tell me. There will always be moments when our *egos*—the parts of us that cling to fear—tell us we are not good enough, that we should be afraid, that we should hide our gifts, that we should dim our lights.

Authenticity isn't about waiting for that fear to disappear. Authenticity means stepping forward into our lights despite the fear. It means choosing to be who we *are*, knowing that not everyone will understand, knowing that some people might walk away, but trusting that the right people—the ones who truly see us—will stay. And those who leave your life? They are making room for those folks who are meant to be with you on the next phase of your journey. But more important, we will show up and love ourselves despite what our egos might tell us.

And *that* is the real freedom.

When I first embraced becoming a medium full-time, I didn't realize that I would have to work through all my own fears, moments of doubt, and feelings of not being enough, of being lacking. In order to communicate with those who have passed, I have to raise my energy to a certain vibration, level, or frequency. To do that, I have to release what is holding me back.

That doesn't mean I don't have my own challenges in life. I still face my own resistance and lessons, but I have learned how to move through them and let them go more quickly so that I can be of service to others. Unfortunately, there is no handbook that gets delivered to you on the day you come out of the spiritual closet.

Authenticity is not just about being yourself. It is about embracing all of who you are, even when it feels uncomfortable, even when the world makes it easier to be someone else. It is about standing in your truth without apologizing, without shrinking, and without needing permission. For a long time, I thought authenticity was something that just happened naturally. If you knew who you were, then being yourself should be easy, right? But what I have learned is that authenticity is a choice you make every single day. It is a commitment to show up as yourself, even when fear tries to convince you that it's safer to play small. It takes courage because the world often rewards people who fit the mold instead of those who break it.

The problem with hiding who you really are is that it does not just protect you from rejection, it also keeps you from real connection. When you are not being fully yourself, the love and acceptance you receive never feel real. Instead, you start wondering if people would still care about you if they knew the truth. You start questioning if you are even worthy of being seen as you are.

Authenticity is about letting go of that fear. It's about realizing that who you are is not something to be ashamed of but something to be proud of. It's about recognizing that the things that make you different are the very things that make you powerful.

When I finally accepted my gift as a medium, I felt the same fear I'd felt when I came out as gay. Would people reject me? Would they call me a fraud? Would I lose the love of the people closest to me? Probably. Most definitely. But what I found was that when I stopped hiding, the right people showed up. The more I stood in my truth, the more my life aligned. The people who were meant to love me stayed. The ones who could not accept me faded away.

That is the gift of authenticity. When you are true to yourself, you create space for the life that is actually meant for you. You attract people who see you, love you, and celebrate you exactly as you are. You stop twisting yourself to fit into spaces that were never meant for you in the first place. Choosing authenticity is not always easy, but I can promise you, it is always worth it.

One of my mentors, MaryAnn DiMarco, once told me, "Speak your truth and all will be revealed to you." I do my best to live by that advice every day. Authenticity does not mean that we always like the way we feel. There are days when I wake up and feel completely alone. It is a familiar loneliness, one I have carried with me since childhood. I do not know exactly when it started or where it came from, but I do know what it means when it shows up. It's a signal that I am disconnected from the whole of who I am.

Authenticity is not about avoiding low-vibrational or negative emotions. Those emotions are beneficial to us, and when embraced they can lead us to massive growth. Spiritual teacher Abraham, who is a collective consciousness channeled through Esther Hicks, refers to them as part of our inner guidance system, which lets us know where we are in relation to where we want to be. What has changed for me over the years is that I no longer try to push those feelings away. I have learned how to take care of myself when they arise. I have come to understand that those feelings are sacred. They are part of me, but they do not define me.

For me, authenticity means knowing that I am not just my physical body. I am not my emotions. I am not my thoughts. I am something greater. Just like the souls of our loved ones who have crossed over, I am energy. I am eternal. The Universe responds to our authenticity. When we show up as ourselves, right where we are, exactly as we are, without trying to fix, change, or run away from ourselves, the Universe meets us where we stand and, in turn, we receive more than we could dream of.

You do not have to be perfect or to have everything figured out. All that the Universe asks is that we just be ourselves. It only asks that we be honest. Honest about our joy. Honest about our struggles. Honest about what we feel, what we need, and what we are still learning. Every time I have chosen to align with my authenticity, my life has shifted in ways I could not have predicted. Life opened up for me. The right opportunities have unfolded. The moments of loneliness, fear, or doubt have passed more quickly because I was not pretending they did not exist. Whenever I was disconnected from that abundance, I was hiding—people-pleasing.

Authenticity is about trust. Trusting that who we are is enough. Trusting that we are loved, even when we feel unworthy. Trusting that we do not have to perform or earn our places in the world. But also trusting ourselves. When we allow ourselves to be seen exactly as we are, we invite the Universe to work with the whole of our energy. And that is when the magic happens.

Authenticity is not just about knowing who you are. It is about choosing to live as that person, even when it is uncomfortable, even when it would be easier to hide. I spent most of my life learning how to shrink myself so other people would accept me. I learned how to be what people needed me to be, how to adjust and perform so I would not stand out too much. But deep down, honey, I always knew I was different. I just didn't know that being different was what gave me my sparkle.

When I first started giving readings, I convinced myself that I was *only* reading tarot. That felt safe. It gave me structure, something to rely on, something to point to when people asked where I was getting my information. The idea of calling myself a medium felt too big, too exposed, too risky. Too honest.

Then, one day, Spirit pushed me forward. Or shoved me, depending on how you look at it.

A Sign

Authenticity isn't just about speaking your truth—it's about *living* it. It's about integrating all you've learned and standing in your integrity, even when it feels uncomfortable. And yes, it can get pretty uncomfortable, but the discomfort is worth the feeling of freedom.

I've learned that the more I step into my authenticity, the more Spirit finds ways to confirm that I'm on the right path. And sometimes, those confirmations show up in ways so undeniable that they stop me in my tracks.

Like when Buck made himself known in a reading.

The moment his name came through, I felt the energy shift. It was strong, clear, unmistakable. His presence was filled with love, and as I relayed his message, I could feel the deep connection he still had with the person I was reading for. It was one of those readings where everything aligned, where Spirit's presence was so tangible that there was no question in my mind—I was exactly where I was meant to be, doing exactly what I was meant to do.

Then later that same day, on a nature walk, I saw *the* buck.

Not just *a* buck—*the* buck.

I wanted to clear my head, but I was also asking the Universe for a sign on how to move forward. I wasn't planning to be a medium forever, at least not at first. And then there he was, the buck. Magnificent and perfect, standing still and powerful with his strong antlers and coat of brown fur, looking right at me, almost as if he understood that he had been placed there just for this moment. Something in me *knew*. This wasn't a coincidence. This wasn't just some random deer sighting. This was a sign. A reminder. A confirmation that Spirit is always speaking, always guiding, always weaving moments of synchronicity into our lives if we're willing to notice them.

The buck wasn't just a symbol of the Spirit I had connected with in the reading—it was also a symbol of my own journey.

Nature doesn't apologize for what it is. A buck doesn't shrink itself to make others comfortable. It stands in its power, fully present, fully *itself*. That moment reminded me that authenticity isn't just about what we say—it's about how we stand in our truths, how we hold our energy, how we trust in what we know to be real.

Because the truth is we are always being guided by Spirit.

Spirit speaks in messages, in synchronicities, in nature, in the undeniable *knowing* we feel when we are in alignment. Living authentically means listening. It means trusting those moments when everything clicks into place. It means paying attention to the signs, not because we need proof, but because they remind us that we are *already* connected, *already* supported, *already* exactly who we are meant to be.

And when we embrace that fully, life opens up in ways we never could have imagined.

Sign received.

TWO

Hello

For a while, I thought my job as a medium was to help people say their final goodbyes. But as I continued facilitating conversations between the physical and nonphysical realms, I realized that that could not be further from the truth. I was not here to bring closure through goodbye—I am here to deliver as many hellos as possible.

Being a medium is like being a radio: I tune in to the frequency of Spirit and receive the broadcast. The more I surrender to the process, the clearer the signal becomes. What an honor it is to facilitate these connections, to remind people that love never dies and to witness the profound healing that happens in those moments of reconnection.

I am a creature of habit. My mornings are sacred to me. I wake up early, meditate, journal, then head to the gym to lift weights.

After that, I come home, eat breakfast, and listen to music, a podcast, or a talk from one of my favorite spiritual teachers on YouTube. It's my morning alignment ritual, and I cherish it immensely.

But one morning, two days after a close friend of mine had passed in her sleep, something felt different. Even though I know that our loved ones are always with us, I felt a pang of regret over not having seen her on my last visit home to Ohio. Her departure was sudden and unexpected, and I felt a very human feeling of guilt for not saying goodbye. As I made my way around my kitchen to make breakfast, I had a thought: *Do we ever truly say goodbye to those we love?* I instinctively reached for my phone and opened my music app. Without thinking much about it, I set it to shuffle, leaving my music selection in the hands of the Universe.

As I placed my phone down and turned to go about my morning, the first few notes of the song that played made me stop mid-step. My friend had loved to sing. She lived for karaoke nights, and of all the songs she performed, my absolute favorite was "Separate Ways (Worlds Apart)" by Journey. And of course—*of course*—that was the very first song, of the more than sixty-eight hundred songs on my phone, that played.

That wasn't a coincidence. That was a hello.

It felt perfectly timed, almost as if the Universe had placed the song in my path as a direct response to my unspoken thoughts.

When someone passes—or even when a relationship ends—we can say goodbye to the physical vessel. We can release the tangible, the form we once knew. But can we ever truly say goodbye to their energy? If we never really say goodbye to the energy of our loved ones, then every sign from our loved ones, every little memory that resurfaces, is not just a remembrance but a gentle hello.

Alexa, Can You Hear Me?

"Hi, honey! It's good to meet you!" I said to my first client of the day. The sky was overcast, the kind of gray, moody weather I love for a day of readings. As I settled into the energy of the client and those who had come forward to communicate, I felt both her parents' energies approaching behind me.

When I connect to loved ones who have crossed over, I feel the energy of the departed come up behind me, much the way you would sense someone in a physical body walk into the room. It starts as a presence, a shift in the air. Then, a chill runs down my back, followed by a sensation in my chest—something between excitement and anxiety. That is how I know it is time. Spirit is ready to chat.

I feel a genuine excitement when I meet my clients for their sessions. Part of it is extreme gratitude for their trust in me and also the anticipation of having no clue as to what is about to happen. Every session has its own nuances and Spirit communicators, which adds a layer of mystery to how the time is going to go. There are very few things I know for absolute certain going into a reading. I only know that Spirit is going to show up and that I'm going to do my absolute best to be the vessel through which they can communicate. Other than that, all bets are off. Sure, I'll get a vague idea of who might come through and what we are going to talk about, but it doesn't become a *knowing* until I'm in the session.

"I'm so grateful to be here with you. Have you ever had a session like this or a reading before?" I always ask this because I like to have a sense of my client's comfort level. Though I'm not sure why, for the most part, the folks who find me have never had a reading before. I then share what they might expect and explain to them how I receive information, whether or not they've had a reading before. If someone is new to me, it's important that they know how I work, even if they are familiar with mediumship or psychic readings.

Every spiritual practitioner is different and has their own style, and mediums have different ways of receiving information. Saying all readings are the same is like saying all books are the same or all movies are the same. My education in mediumship has provided a framework, but that framework has allowed me to develop my own methods of delivery and receiving that are constantly evolving and changing.

This particular client had received several mediumship sessions in the past. I didn't ask about them; I prefer to keep the client's energy grounded in the present moment, and reflecting on a past experience can pull that energy away. Mediumship is at its best when all parties are grounded in the here and now. It's a three-way connection: Spirit, the client, and me. Since Spirit is eternally present, it's up to me and the sitter (the person receiving the messages) to keep our energy focused right where we are. Major distractions or shifts in energy can cause a break in the link between me and the soul of the Spirit communicator. It's simple to reconnect, but I enjoy being in the flow with Spirit.

We began the reading, and I felt something I don't usually feel before a session: My whole body was tingling. And it wasn't a light, warm, fuzzy tingling. I felt I was filled with electricity that was looking for a place to flow. I wiggled my feet into the floor to ground myself again—a technique one of my mentors taught me to help my body relax—and to allow the energy to smooth out. Both the woman's parents, her mom's and dad's energies, felt as though they were standing behind me.

"I have your mom here and also your dad."

My client smiled. "Hi, Mom. Hi, Dad," she said softly. Her parents had been departed for the majority of her life, and she believed she had a deep connection with them in Spirit already. They then handed me balloons, and I felt there was cause for celebration.

"Okay, they are giving me balloons. Is it your birthday?" And it was! I love birthdays, and Spirit usually makes me aware of birthdays pretty early on in my sessions. I believe this is because they want us to know that they are with us celebrating, even if we don't see them.

"My most recent memory of them is celebrating my birthday. I haven't been able to celebrate my birthday since they died," she told me. I could feel her grief and deep longing for her parents to be there to help celebrate her special day. "How do they feel about their deaths?" she asked me.

Until that point, no one had ever asked me what their loved one's soul felt about passing on.

All right, you heard her. How do you feel about your transitions?

Her mom spoke up first. *It's like the day you are born. It's a celebration of one part of the journey ending and another part beginning.*

I shared this with my client, and she smiled.

"That would be my mom. Classic. Mom wasn't afraid of dying. Even when she was sick, she reminded me that we keep going."

Physical birth and physical death are just markers on that never-ending cable of eternity my youth minister had told me about. They are the beginning and end points on that razor-thin slice, nothing more. Yet even though the journey in this physical body is short, it's also incredibly special—and worthy of celebration.

As the session continued, messages flowed in gently, delivering reassurance that my client's loved ones were indeed nearby and continuing to watch over her. Then, as we were finishing up, I can only describe what happened next as a miracle. And though I see miracles every day, each one of them incredibly special, this one carried such a powerful energy that I can only describe it as a miracle with some extra sparkle.

"Travis, I really enjoyed our time together," my client told me. "All I wanted was to hear my parents say hello one more time."

Suddenly, we were both startled to hear a voice say hello.

I usually close my office door when I see clients, but on this day I'd left the door open, and the door to my bedroom across the hall was also open. I realized that the voice belonged to the Alexa device in the bedroom.

My client and I stared at each other.

"Who just said hello?" my client asked.

"Hello." Again Alexa was saying hello, and this time even louder and clearer than before.

"Well, that would be my Alexa, but it's all the way in my bedroom. I can't say I've ever had that happen before!"

"Hello." Again. Another hello from the Alexa in my bedroom.

"Honey, this is the strangest thing I've ever had happen during a reading," I told her.

Could her parents have been saying hello through Alexa? And if so, how could that be possible? I tried to stay present and not let my mind overthink it too much, but this felt like more than just a coincidence. I also wondered if I was losing my mind. Thankfully, my client heard the voice, too.

"The strange thing is," she began, "ever since the day I scheduled my appointment with you, my Alexa has been saying hello off and on."

In that moment, I knew that what we were experiencing was very real. And though I didn't know exactly how this was happening, I didn't really need to know. I felt chills running through my body. I could feel the energy of her departed parents in a way I hadn't felt a Spirit communicator before. I wiggled my feet into the floor again.

"It sounds like your parents knew exactly what you needed," I said.

After we finished the session, I sat at my desk, staring at the space in front of me, trying to wrap my head around what had just happened. I had experienced many mediumistic moments growing up—countless, really—and every single one felt real to me. But this? This was different.

There was a power behind it that I had never felt before. It felt as if I'd stuck my finger in a spiritual light socket. The sensation was so palpable, so undeniable, that I found myself lingering in the energy, reluctant to let it fade. Even though the direct connection with the woman's parents had ended, their presence still lingered. The air around me felt charged, electric. The hairs on my arms stood on end, my body tingled from head to toe, and I could feel the energy buzzing in the space around me.

I sat still, doing my best to ground myself, imagining the energy moving through me—flowing down my spine, through my legs, and out through my feet into the floor beneath me. But even that didn't help. It was as if I was floating—caught between heaven and Earth, lingering in the thin vibrational space between the seen and unseen.

I needed to make sense of what had happened. I got up, walked into my bedroom, and went straight to my Alexa. I picked it up, examined the cords, and tested its sensitivity. I wanted to see if something—anything—could have triggered it. I waved my hand in front of it, moved around the room, adjusted the settings, and tried to re-create the moment. I said, "Alexa," out loud—several times, in fact—and got absolutely no response from the device.

Nothing.

Now, let me be clear: I have never questioned the work that I do. I more than believe in the continuation of life beyond this physical experience; I *know* we continue on. A belief is something that leaves room for us to change our minds or have doubt, and mediumship isn't something I wonder about. I *know* it's real. I know that our loved ones in Spirit are always communicating with us. I know that the Universe is always responding to our energy. What I used to wonder was if I was worthy enough to deliver these messages from Spirit.

That day, something shifted for me. Because of the intensity of this experience, my belief in my own worthiness deepened. I didn't quite *know* I was worthy, but I believed it just a little more than I did when I woke up that morning. Sometimes just having a little more belief than we did yesterday can help us make our way to knowing.

I don't believe that our loved ones in Spirit have a mission to prove to us that they're there. They remind us—again and again—of their presence. But more important, they remind us that we are not alone and that we are worthy of receiving messages and signs from them.

Because we are. And we always have been.

The Loneliness

Loneliness is something I have felt for as long as I can remember. It has followed me throughout my life, sometimes subtly, sometimes overwhelmingly. But when I'm giving readings?

I don't feel lonely at all.

In those moments, I feel deeply connected—not just to the person in front of me, and not just to their loved ones in Spirit, but to *everything*. To life itself. To the great unseen. And more than anything, to *myself*. There's a Brené Brown quote that has always stuck with me: "Spirituality is recognizing and celebrating that we are inextricably connected to each other by a power greater than all of us." And I believe that is what our loved ones in Spirit remind us when they come through with evidence of their existence beyond the physical world. They are not just showing us that they are still connected to us, seeing everything we do and taking interest in what we would consider the most mundane aspects of our existence—they are showing us that *we* are still connected to them, as well.

The Universe is always offering us opportunities to remember that connection. Not just the connection we have with our loved ones who have transitioned, but the connection we have with ourselves—the part of us that is also deeply tied to a power greater than us.

Through that connection, we create our lives. And to take it a step further, beyond Spirit and us, it allows us to connect more deeply with our fellow humans.

When we feel grief, what we're really feeling is a lack of connection.

When we feel scarcity, we're feeling a lack of connection.

When we feel loneliness, we're feeling a lack of connection.

The opposite of love is not hate. The opposite of love is *disconnection* from love.

And if disconnection is the wound, *connection* is the medicine.

The Universe, in all its wisdom and love, is constantly showing us—nudging us, whispering to us, wrapping around us in ways big and small—just how transformative and healing the power of connection truly is.

The Bad (?) Date

In my personal life, I was looking for another type of connection. I had made the conscious decision to start dating. I felt incredibly satisfied with my life and where I was on my journey, but I couldn't shake the feeling that perhaps something could be added into the mix. While I wasn't certain if I was ready personally to be in a long-term, heavily committed relationship, I was craving connection beyond the connection I already had in my life. If you've ever tried dating apps, then you know how interesting they can be. The Universe can work miracles—anywhere, even on dating apps.

A few days after the reading with the client when Alexa said hello, I met someone through an app, and we agreed to have a dinner date. For the sake of privacy, I'll call this individual Tom.

Tom worked in the tech industry, more specifically in data security. We arranged to meet at a local Mexican restaurant, and after a long day of sessions, I was excited to shift my energy to conversations about those here in the living.

I walked into the restaurant to find Tom already seated in a booth. As soon as I sat down, he hit me with the question I'd dreaded—so much so that I'm sure my reluctance to answer it contributed to my anxieties around dating. No hello. No *How are you?*

"What do you do for work?" he asked me.

I'm not ashamed of the work I do. In fact, I'm incredibly proud of it. At the time, though, I worried about what other people thought of me. Silly, right? Well, sweetheart, when we have histories of being rejected for who we are, we create subconscious barriers that keep us from connection. I had built emotional walls so high, afraid of vulnerability and connection, that it would have taken a small army to break those walls down.

"I'm a medium." The tone of my voice went flat, and I forced a smile. He stared at me, so I followed up with, "You know . . . like, a psychic medium?"

"No, you're not. That's not real." Again, Tom was direct, and in a way, I appreciated it. Most people won't tell you what they truly think of you, and here was Tom just saying what he was thinking.

"Oh . . . Well, damn, I guess I should go tell my Instagram followers," I joked. Tom did not smile. He just stared at me, barely moving aside from an occasional blinking of his eyes.

"So, Tom, what do you love about your job?" I asked, hoping to shift the conversation to something that had absolutely nothing to do with my being a medium.

"I love that I work with computers all day. But what you do isn't real."

Now, look, I don't pay Tom's bills, and I don't really care what Tom believes for himself. But as he spoke, I could feel something stirring inside me—memories I hadn't thought about in a long time. Memories tied to doubt and shame. Memories of growing up feeling like I had to prove I was worthy. I wanted to be angry, but what I actually felt was something much deeper—a familiar ache, an emptiness of *not enough*.

I didn't even know Tom, and yet I found myself wanting his approval. And that's when I remembered my session with the client earlier in the week. How undeniable the connection had been. How deeply I had felt Spirit. I took a breath and let the knowing settle back into my body. I was enough.

No matter what this man sitting across from me thought.

He could be a skeptic. He could not believe in what I do. But that didn't change who *I* was. It didn't diminish my truth, my experiences, or my work.

So I sat up a little taller, met his gaze, and shared my truth.

I told him that I believe we are all energy. That people who are psychics and mediums simply have the ability to tune in to that energy in a different way. It doesn't make us better, just different—in the way that some people are naturally gifted at math or music, or in Tom's case, technology. I told him how I, personally, have no talent for technology, but that doesn't make me *less than*—just different.

And when I finished, I was certain that my words hadn't changed a thing for him. That he would still be skeptical and unmoved. But that didn't matter. Because I had spoken from the heart.

"Fine. Then give me a reading," Tom said, still direct.

I smiled. "I don't think so." His eyebrows raised slightly.

"You see, Tom, I don't give readings to people I go on dates with. That's a boundary of mine because I want to have my own experience with you. Also, while I welcome skepticism, your complete lack of belief would stand in the way the entire time. You'd block the experience before it even started."

He smirked slightly. "Yeah. Okay."

He changed the subject.

We moved through the rest of dinner—Tom tossing questions my way, my answering and asking my own in the hope of finding some kind of meaningful connection. But I could tell that he wasn't really interested in anything beyond surface-level conversation. It started to feel less like a date and more like a full-blown CIA interrogation.

And yet, when I look back on that night, I smile. Because that date was a moment when I could have shrunk myself. I could have given in to his request, tried to prove myself, let his skepticism trigger my own doubt. But I didn't. Because at that table, I knew there was *nothing lacking*. Not even Tom's lack of faith because his beliefs were perfect as they were. It wasn't my job to convince him of anything. His beliefs were *his* journey—just as my gifts were mine.

And in that moment, it became so clear to me: I needed to be with someone who believed in what I do. Not just with someone who tolerated it. Or with someone who didn't mind it. Someone who *believed*—because my work, my connection to Spirit, isn't something I can separate from myself. It's part of *who I am*. Just like being gay is a part of me. Just like being sparkly is. I can't change it. And I *don't want to*.

I have this ability for a reason—to help people find connection, to remind them of the love that exists beyond this physical world, and to make them aware of their own lights. And while I do believe that my mediumship ability is just that—an ability—I also believe that what I *choose* to do with it is a *gift*. And that gift isn't just for the people I serve. It's for me, too.

Because this work has led me into a deeper connection with my own soul.

"So would you like to go on a second date?" Tom asked. I blinked. *Were we on the same date?!*

That dinner was no great date. But Tom had given me a gift that night—I learned a lot about myself. Our dinner was a reminder that *exactly who I am is exactly who I need to be*. I now knew that I never had to shrink myself for the sake of someone else's approval. Still, a second date was not in the cards.

"Out of curiosity, why do you want to have a second date with me?" I asked, genuinely curious.

"It's hard to meet people. And you seem all right."

I knew what he meant. I had been kind. I had shown him respect. I had held space for him while still honoring myself. But I also knew that wasn't enough. So I politely declined and wished him the best on his search. I left the table feeling more whole than when I'd sat down. Thank you, Tom.

As I stepped outside, the sky was painted with the soft golds and pinks of a setting sun, and a warm breeze wrapped around me. I decided to take a stroll around the neighborhood, soaking in the quiet of the evening. As I walked, I thought about *connection*. The kind I had with friends. With my parents. With Spirit. With the people I serve. All these relationships were different, all were at varying depths, but all were still *love*. And then a thought hit me like a wave: I already had what I was looking for. It didn't look the way I thought it would, but love was everywhere in my life. I wasn't missing anything. I had more than enough.

And more important, I was finally beginning to cultivate a deeper connection with myself. I knew there were still things to heal, layers to peel back, and ways I would need to grow before I could fully receive the type of relationship I desired.

But for now, in this moment, I had everything I needed.

Because here's the thing about desires: They exist within us because they are *possible*. The word *desire* comes from the Latin *de sidere*, which means "from the stars." Those desires that are deep within you, that light you up when you think about them and feel expansive and joyful? They were given to you by the Universe for you to experience. And the Universe will not give you a desire that cannot be fulfilled.

The Universe has already set into motion the chain of events that will allow you to actualize your desires. Our job isn't to chase after them—it's to clear anything standing in their way and prepare ourselves to receive. And as we do, life gives us little nudges, little reminders—showing us where we've closed ourselves off, where we've built walls that block us. But the Universe always provides a way to reopen our hearts, and our beliefs, to the possibility of more.

To remind us that connection is *always* available.

That even when we feel alone, we are *never* truly disconnected.

And as I walked, lost in those thoughts, allowing myself to become fully aware of what I desired next, my eye caught something spray-painted on a nearby brick wall. One simple word.

HELLO.

I laughed to myself, shaking my head.

Another wink from the Universe.

Because the connection is always there—if we're open to seeing it. And even though I desired more, I also realized that what I had

HELLO

in this moment was enough. I felt complete. I knew there would be more times when I would feel that deep loneliness. But I also had a knowing that I could make my way to feeling just a little better, and all I needed to do was reach out and say hello.

THREE

Trust Fall

There's something that happens when you step into being a medium professionally—something no one can truly prepare you for. And it's not the late-night visits from Spirit, the sudden waves of energy at inconvenient moments, or even the deep knowings I sometimes wish I *didn't know*.

It's the *healing*.

The kind of healing that unfolds within you, even as you dedicate yourself to helping others heal. No one tells you just how much of yourself you'll see reflected in the messages you deliver. How often Spirit will hold up a mirror and say, *Look. Here's where you're still holding pain. Here's where you still have work to do.*

Every teacher and mentor predicted that this would happen for me. They told me that mediumship isn't just about delivering messages—it's about growth, transformation, and healing, not only for those I serve but for me. And yet, even with all their guidance, I still had no idea what I was in for. Imagine walking a tightrope suspended high above the ground. Every step forward is a balance of confidence, faith, and surrender. If you focus too much on fear, you freeze. If you try to control every movement, you wobble. But when you trust the rope, your training, and the unseen forces holding you up, you find your rhythm. Mediumship is no different, and neither is self-healing.

To connect with Spirit, you must trust what you receive, even when doubt creeps in. You must quiet the noise of skepticism, ego, and expectation and allow something beyond your logical mind to flow through you. The more you try to force the experience, the more you block it. But when you surrender, open up, and trust in what you are receiving, the messages flow with ease. You become the bridge—or the high wire—between two worlds.

Self-healing also requires this delicate balance of belief and surrender. Healing isn't about fixing yourself, because you aren't broken; it's about remembering your wholeness. It's about allowing light to pour into the places where you once only saw darkness. Healing asks you to trust that, even in your most uncertain moments, there is something greater guiding you. Just as a tightrope walker must trust that each step forward will hold, you must trust that your growth, your healing, and your transformation are already unfolding.

All these things require courage, but courage doesn't always come naturally. Sometimes, we need a little support or the knowledge that there's a place for us to land if we lose our balance. When we take that trust fall, we tell the Universe, *I'm ready to fly, and I trust that I will also have a place to land.*

Existential Crisis on a Dance Floor

Some of my most cherished moments have happened on a dance floor. I found safety in them at the age of fifteen. My first club experience was in Ohio, and at the time, it was one of the most magical things I had ever experienced. Ever since then, dance floors have been spaces of sacred movement for me. Moving my body to the rhythm of the music, releasing doubt and fear, and experiencing the intoxicating power of being fully present in my body—even more so when my closest friends surround me—is unlike anything else. Some people are terrified of being on dance floors, but I run to them.

But this one particular evening, as I looked around the crowded club at couples dancing together, touching, I began to panic.

"Do you think I'm guarded from love?" I asked my friend Will over the sound of electronic music and heavy bass. It was a Saturday night a few weeks after the date with Tom, and I was having an existential crisis on the dance floor.

"I don't know if you're guarded from love, but I do think you might choose relationships that feel predictable to keep from getting hurt," Will replied, knowing I did not want him to hold back. Will is not the kind of friend who gives unsolicited advice, but if you ask him a question, he'll be completely honest.

"So that's a yes," I said, laughing even though I knew he was right.

I had not been in a relationship for a few years and had recently decided I wanted to start dating again. But the thought of it brought up so much fear and apprehension. On one hand, I wanted to meet someone, to share in the kind of love I saw my friends experiencing. On the other hand, I was terrified of the pain that comes with loss. By my mid-thirties, I thought I would have human relationships mastered by now, but I was finding that I had more questions than answers.

Some people think mediums, psychics, and the like have it all figured out. The truth is we don't. Or, at least, I don't. I'm working through my own lessons, just like everyone else. I am out in this world, dating and looking for a partner. I am not immune to life lessons, nor do I get an easy pass. Because of the work I do, I believe it's even more important for me to learn my own lessons. If I can't learn them for myself, how on earth can I help others walk through theirs?

So there I was, on the dance floor, usually my comfort zone and haven, having an existential crisis in the company of my friends. As I looked around the room at the couples holding hands, I thought, *That would be so nice to have.* It would be nice to have someone I loved, cared for, and adored—and someone who loved, cared for, and adored me, too. Like many people, I grew up on Disney and rom-coms, and I fell for the lie that there is someone out there who will complete you. While I do not believe that anymore, I could not ignore the lonely pang in my chest whispering, *When will I meet someone?* The loneliness was back.

The Healers Also Need Healers

I started therapy a few years ago when my drinking was spiraling out of control and my self-esteem was at an all-time low. I was afraid my therapist would think I was absurd when I told him I was a medium and that I talk to those in Spirit—my past therapists had been judgmental when I shared vulnerable parts of myself. But when I told Michael, he didn't even flinch. He simply asked a few questions about how I hear and see Spirit, and that was that. I described my evening at the club to him in detail and told him that one of my closest friends had said I might choose predictable relationships to avoid getting hurt.

"Well, do you feel that's true?" he asked, closing his hands together and waiting for my response.

"Ugh. I mean, yeah, I do think it's partially true, but there's another part that I haven't admitted to myself yet," I said. "Do I deserve to receive love?" The words fell out of my mouth, and suddenly, my mind was filled with questions. *Am I worthy of love? What if I receive love and then lose it?* That was my deepest fear of all, and I had just said it out loud for the first time. I could feel tears forming in my eyes.

For a long time, I'd been carrying the belief that love was not something I deserved, and definitely not something I deserved to keep. The energy of that belief sat heavy in my chest, like a rock lodged in my heart. No matter what I did, I couldn't seem to shake it. No affirmation, no logical thought could remove this dense weight of feeling unworthy of love.

No wonder dating felt like such a struggle.

"When do you feel worthy?" Michael asked me, his voice soft and steady.

"Well, I guess I think I'm worthy," I said, my voice raising in pitch the way it does when I'm uncomfortable.

By now, Michael could always tell when I was unsure of myself. Hell, *I* could tell when I was unsure of myself.

"No, when do you *feel* it?" he asked. "It's one thing to think it, but it's another to really feel it."

"When I'm in sessions with clients and connected to Spirit—that's when I feel worthy. That's when I feel whole." More tears. I had not said that out loud yet, either.

For as long as I could remember, I had felt this hole inside of me. Nothing ever seemed to fill it. In my twenties and early thirties, I tried everything: drugs, food, sex, overworking, binge drinking, seeking validation. But nothing worked. It was like shoveling endless distractions into the void, only to feel empty again.

But when I connect to Spirit in a session with a client, I feel full. Genuinely full. I don't feel I need to prove anything. I feel peace in my entire body. On days when my energy is low, I always feel better by the end of my sessions. That's because connecting to Spirit is connecting to love. It is a state of peace where there is no lack, no suffering—only clarity. I believe we can all experience this.

Surrender is one of the hardest lessons Spirit has ever asked me to learn. It's easy to trust when everything is going the way we want, when signs are showing up, when opportunities are flowing, and when life feels like it's working in our favor. But real trust happens in the moments when nothing makes sense. When doors close. When plans fall apart. When fear creeps in and tells us we should turn back.

For a long time, I thought surrender meant giving up. I thought it meant being passive, sitting back, and waiting for something to magically happen. But surrender is not about quitting. It is about allowing. It is about understanding that we are never fully in control and that no amount of forcing, overthinking, or worrying is going to make something happen faster or in a different way than it is meant to happen.

Spirit does not operate on human timelines. That has been one of my biggest lessons. I've had moments when I begged for clarity, for certainty, for answers right away, only to be met with silence. What I've learned is that silence is not abandonment. It is space. It is Spirit inviting me to trust, to lean into the unknown, and to allow things to unfold in their own time.

Surrender is like a trust fall with the Universe. It asks us to let go of the need to control and trust that something greater is at work. Every time I've let go, Spirit has caught me. Every time I've released my grip on what I thought *should* happen, something better has come along.

The Universe always has a plan. Our job is not to micromanage it. Our job is to trust.

Maybe that was what I needed, to lean into the belief that I was worthy of love even when I was met with silence. To take a leap, not knowing where I would land. Maybe I needed that space of silence to allow myself to fully step into surrender. I trusted Spirit and myself enough to deliver messages to others. Could I trust myself enough to be in the uncomfortable space of silence and open up to the possibility of love?

Is This Thing On?

A few weeks later, I found myself on a plane headed to Denver. There is a wonderful spiritual community based there called Awkwardly Zen, and the founder, Ari, invited me to come out and do a live mediumship demonstration at a local distillery. A mediumship demonstration is when a medium gathers with a group of people and delivers messages to individuals in the audience. I had never done something like this in front of a live crowd, only through Zoom. While I was uncertain about how it would all unfold, I knew that when Spirit nudged me to do something, it was always for my own growth.

The thing with nudges from Spirit is that they do not always mean that the path will be smooth. That's where leaning into surrender gets uncomfortable for a lot of people. It's easy to surrender and trust when everything is sunshine and rainbows. It's a whole other story when we are experiencing difficulty. But that's the whole point, to trust even when the road is bumpy or there is turbulence.

"Are you ready?" Ari asked, her hands gently resting on my shoulders, grounding me in the moment.

You should know something about Ari. Her energy is unlike that of anyone I have ever met. The only word that comes close to capturing her essence is *angelic*. Being around her feels like stepping into a calm, warm embrace. She carries a radiance that is not just seen but felt, a quiet light that seems to wrap around you with every word she speaks.

"Ready as I'm ever going to be."

As she left the private area in the back of the distillery where I was taking time to prepare, a flash of heat consumed my body. Suddenly, my hands began to tremble, and I felt nauseated. Could it be stage fright? That was highly unlikely. I was a theater kid in high school and had performed at drag shows through most of my late teens and twenties. I loved being onstage. It felt like a second home to me. There was no way I was nervous.

Then I started to cry in panic. "I can't do this!" I said aloud into the void. *Maybe I can run out the back door?* I thought. Breathing deeply, I went into the bathroom backstage to hide and called my friend Lo for reinforcement.

"Lo, I think I'm having a panic attack," I told her.

"Where are you?" she asked, concerned.

"I'm crying in the bathroom backstage before I have to go out and give readings to a room full of people, and I don't think I can do this," I said into the phone.

Lo is a soul sister, someone I met when I worked in the beauty industry. From the moment we met, I knew she was family.

"Okay, listen, Trav, you can do this. I believe in you. You are Travis Holp. You are here to help people. Now go out there and help people."

And she was right. I was there to help people. I was not there to prove myself or make the event all about my fear and ego. Spirit had opened this door for me to deliver healing messages to those who had come to the distillery that evening, and I was going to show up on that stage and surrender, or at least try.

The next thing I knew, I could hear Ari announcing my name to the crowd, and it was time to go onstage. I stepped onto the small platform in front of fifty people, nervous and unsure of what was about to happen. The moment my foot touched the wooden stage, I felt a tidal wave of energy. It was like stepping onto a crowded subway platform, incredibly noisy with the feeling of energy rushing all around me. Although the audience was silent, inside my head was chaotic with all the chatter.

My daughter is here!

My brother is on the left side of the room!

My ex-wife is in the back!

The different voices were all shouting for my attention. I felt like I was treading water. My heart was racing, and sweat was dripping down my back.

Well, this is it . . . I thought.

I began by telling the audience who I am and what to expect for the evening, which is always the unexpected. Truthfully, even *I* had no idea what to expect. My hands were shaking as I started receiving information from those in the nonphysical realm who came to relay messages. I looked directly at a woman close to the back row and shared bits of information that were coming through, like his name, his passing, but it didn't feel like the steady flow of information I typically receive. This was more clunky, almost like tiny drips of information. And then . . . nothing.

The room was completely silent—an excruciating silence. *Kiss your career goodbye, honey,* I thought to myself. Very seldom did I ever find myself blocked or receiving information that didn't connect, but there I was on the podium sharing information about a Spirit communicator, and nothing was resonating with the person I was looking at. If I could have fled the stage and crawled into a hole, I would have.

After a few more minutes of dead air (pun intended) I decided it would be best to move on. I began to build momentum as the next few readings seemed to hold meaning for those in the room. One by one, I delivered messages to those in the audience, eventually connecting to a mother trying to reach her daughter. The mother and the daughter weren't on speaking terms at the time of the mother's passing.

"She wants you to know that she's sorry. I know that doesn't make up for her absence, but she is acknowledging where she fell short for you." I could feel my body flood with the feeling of remorse—not that we carry remorse with us when we pass on, but Spirit will share feelings in my body that help convey the message that needs to be delivered. The daughter receiving the message began to cross her arms, and I knew this was not exactly the message she wanted to hear. (It's my belief that when it comes to mediumship and receiving messages, we don't always hear what we want to hear, but it's almost always what we need to hear.)

As I stood on the stage, I noticed that my body had relaxed, and my energy was more open. *You've got this*, I heard a voice say. The voice was very familiar, as it was the voice of my Spirit Guide. *Thank you*, I replied silently, and then asked for something specific that I could mention to the daughter of the mother who was still very much sharing with me that because of their relationship, her daughter had a hard time trusting and opening up to people close to her. She had become guarded and afraid to open her heart out of fear of being abandoned again. *Please mention the sunflower tattoo*, I heard the mother say.

"Honey, Mom wants me to mention the sunflower tattoo."

The young woman just stared at me. The ten seconds of stillness felt like an eternity. Had I missed again? No. She was removing her cardigan to reveal a sunflower tattoo on her shoulder. Folks around her gasped, and I asked her to stand and please show the audience the tattoo. She began to get emotional, and I delivered words that came from her mother, a heartfelt message of channeled wisdom from her mother's soul self.

"Your mom is letting me know that it's time to open your heart again. Because of your relationship with her, you've learned to be mistrustful—to guard yourself, to protect yourself from being hurt. And I get it. But, sweetheart, here's what I know to be true: When we close off our hearts, we don't just protect ourselves from pain—we also block ourselves from possibility. We shut out the amazing things life has in store for us. And, maybe most importantly, we cut ourselves off from a deeper connection with *ourselves*. Whether you desire a romantic relationship or simply want to foster deeper connections with the people around you, keeping your heart closed makes that nearly impossible. Because *who you are*—at your core—is a heart-centered being. I don't have words that can erase what happened between you and your mom. But what I *can* tell you is this: You are here, right now, in this physical life, with the power to shape your future. You can't change what happened to you. But you *can* decide how you move forward."

I took a deep breath. The feeling that moved through my body felt like electricity; I had never experienced a flow of information like that before from a Spirit communicator.

The young woman smiled. "Thank you so much for that message," she said. "I didn't realize how much I needed it."

And what she didn't realize was that I needed that message, too.

It doesn't happen often, but every once in a while a reading reflects to me lessons I'm also navigating in my own life, where messages I share for someone else feel like they're meant for me, too. Like the young woman in the audience that night who spoke about a challenging relationship with her mother, one that had caused her to close off her heart to the possibility of deeper connections. I could see myself in her story. I had been there once, too.

In that moment, I realized something profound: The healing wasn't one sided. It hit me that mediumship isn't just about giving; it's also about receiving, often in ways we don't even know we need. That night, Spirit worked through me for both of us.

After the event, I checked in with my Spirit Guides to see how I could have better prepared in order not to have been bombarded by the energy. We all have Spirit Guides, and they are nonphysical energies that are here to help us in this lifetime. They can come in many different forms, such as angels, ancestors, even animals. I like to think of mine as energy that I can feel and sense that helps me find clarity on my path and helps guide my intuition.

You didn't ask for help, I heard my Guide say. When I say I can hear my Guides, it's usually in my own thought voice, not a separate voice. It starts as a high-pitched frequency that my brain then interprets into a thought. I know when it's my Guide or my intuition because the communication is very direct. There's little to no emotion, and I feel in my body the alignment with what's being said, even if it isn't what I want to hear. It's like when a friend gives you advice, and you know it's accurate but it isn't quite what you are wanting.

"Well, aren't we sassy today!" I said aloud as I sat on the floor, having a conversation with the energy in the room. I talk to my Guides the way I talk to my friends; my Guides know me, and they certainly don't expect formality.

"What could I have asked for help with?" I said. Almost immediately, I was shown the scene of me walking onstage, being flooded by energy.

You could just specify how you want the information delivered to you.

While that made logical sense to me, I had another thought. "Well, shouldn't you just know? . . . I mean, you are my Guides," I asked. And what came next I should have seen coming.

You have free will. The purpose is not for us to intervene but to assist when asked. You have to be open and ready to receive.

And there it was. The lesson about trust and keeping my heart open. I had been so used to doing things on my own and shouldering all the responsibility myself that asking for help didn't even cross my mind.

Back for More

A few short months later, Ari invited me back to Denver for another event, but this time, it would be for 150 people. And this time, I knew that I had help from my Guides and from friends here in the physical world. Some of my closest friends had flown to Denver to support me during this next mediumship demonstration. As I waited backstage to be announced, I gave my Guides clear instructions on how I wanted to receive information, and I expressed my deepest gratitude for allowing me the honor of delivering messages from loved ones who have left this physical earth. My Guides' energy was all around me. At that moment, I heard, *If you get nervous, just look into the audience.* With that, it was time for me to deliver messages.

That evening, the presence of Spirit was undeniable—almost electric. With each message, the room pulsed with an energy that felt both expansive and deeply healing, wrapping everyone in its embrace. Anytime a flicker of nervousness crept in, I'd glance over at my incredible friends, who had shown up for me in this huge moment.

Lo; Will and his husband, Siy; Zach with his new boyfriend, Ed; Matthew. My chosen family—built over years of love, laughter, and unwavering connection—were there cheering me on, their presence as steady as ever. It felt like they were watching me take a leap off a bungee platform—sending me all the love in the world but also knowing, deep down, that I had the strength to take the jump on my own. Their belief in me, paired with the undeniable flow of Spirit, made the night one I'll never forget.

Friends are like Spirit Guides in human form, and I truly believe our Guides often work through them—nudging them to say exactly what we need to hear, exactly when we need to hear it. Or sometimes their presence can simply be enough to anchor you in the vibration of love.

That night was magical because I allowed myself to trust. Not just to trust Spirit but to trust the people who had shown up for me. When nerves crept in, I didn't have to carry them alone. I was supported—by the physical presence of my friends and by the unseen guidance of Spirit, both working in harmony.

But the biggest revelation came in a quiet moment of realization: The same bravery that had allowed me to open myself to Spirit could also help me open my heart to love. If I could take the leap to receive Spirit and share its healing with a room full of people, then surely I could take the leap to let someone in.

That's what a trust fall *really* is—taking a leap without knowing exactly where you'll land but choosing to jump anyway. Those big leaps in life can be terrifying—whether it's putting yourself out there for the world to truly see you, making a bold career move, allowing yourself to heal, or opening your heart to love.

Certainty of the outcome isn't always part of the equation. But maybe that's the beauty of it. The real gift is when the possibility of growth, connection, and expansion becomes more exciting than the fear that's been keeping you frozen in place. Fear will never fully disappear. It's part of being human. And there's never a promise of success. But we can choose to amplify our joy—to let it be louder than the fear—so it doesn't keep us closed off from the possibilities that are waiting for us.

I knew there was healing I needed to do before I could fully receive the relationship I desired. But for the first time, I wasn't afraid to take the leap. Because I knew that no matter what happened . . . I had a place to land.

FOUR

The Heart of the Matter

"What are you noticing, Travis?" The therapist's voice was calm and grounding, guiding me as I sat on the gray sofa in her intimate office overlooking Seattle. The sun was coming through one of the windowpanes, pouring warmth into the room. A steady *click, click, click* was coming from the speaker of her computer, anchoring my energy in the room.

I was in an EMDR therapy session. EMDR stands for eye movement desensitization and reprocessing. It's a type of therapy that helps you reprocess traumatic experiences that get stuck in the mind and body like old ghosts. I suppose you could say that the only haunting I'd experienced was my own past. I was there to work through traumatic memories I had held on to from the events that had taken place when I came out to my family.

Like a lot of kids who grew up in the Midwest with conservative families, I experienced quite the ordeal when I came out. My mother, whom I have a wonderful relationship with now, didn't know how to respond to having a gay child. Fear, misunderstanding, and societal conditioning got the best of her, and the fallout left wounds on both sides.

Coming out for me was a painful experience because I knew how my family felt about gay people. I had a great relationship with my mom and Nanan, and I knew that by coming out, those relationships would be strained at best and destroyed at worst. The people I loved the most were also the people I feared the most.

But it was becoming more difficult to hide the fact that I was gay, and I couldn't stay in a closet any longer. The fear of losing my family became less than the fear of being somebody that I was not. When I finally told my family, it was worse than I could have imagined. My mom had an extremely emotional reaction and called my grandmother over to help. To help do what, exactly? I'm not sure. Help convince me that I wasn't gay, perhaps? As I sat on the therapist's couch, she gently guided me back to the memory of what it was like to come out. As I began to recall the memory, I could feel my heart race. I could see my mother's face and the disappointment and fear in her eyes. I could hear my grandmother saying that I was going to hell. I could feel their anger and disappointment, but above all I could feel their fear.

"What are you seeing? What are you feeling?" the therapist said, her soothing voice feeling like a safety rope as I dove deep into a repressed memory.

"Mom is crying, and so is my grandmother. My grandmother keeps calling me sick in the head."

"Where are you feeling that in your body?" she asked, and I began to explain the sensations that I was experiencing throughout my chest. And then I felt my body begin to contract, almost instinctively recoil into a ball so that I would not be seen. I suddenly felt afraid all over again, as if the event were happening in real time. I could feel myself in the body of my younger self, crouched in a corner crying while Mom yelled. My mom and dad were divorced by then, and so it was just my mom taking care of me and my sister. My mother's support through all of this was her mother, Nanan, who also was not prepared to hear my truth.

At that moment during therapy, I suddenly remembered my nanan suggesting I be sent away. The memory of her and my mom both saying that I couldn't be around my family, especially my sister, replayed like a horrible movie, and I was right in the middle of it. My sister and I had always been close, and the idea of not seeing her again terrified me.

I could feel myself being abandoned all over again. It didn't feel like a past event, it felt as if it were happening right here in the present moment. My heart was beating fast, and my body was so tense. I could hear my mom and Nanan yelling and crying and my younger sister crying for them to stop. The room felt like it was closing in on me, and it was becoming difficult to breathe.

"If you could tell your younger self something in this moment, what would it be?" the therapist said, and I began to visualize myself standing in front of the younger me in this memory. It was a calm moment in the midst of chaos. I hugged little me and told him that he was safe. He was safe, and what was happening wasn't okay. He asked me if we would ever be okay, and all I could say to him was "Eventually." I told him that I would protect him, and that he would be able to live a life that was completely his, and that one day, Mom, Dad, and Sister would be incredibly supportive of him. I told him that in this moment, even though I was terrified, it had nothing to do with his, with my, worthiness.

The session concluded, and I felt that a giant wound had been reopened so it could heal properly. Previously, I had leaned into drugs and alcohol to try to numb the loneliness that emerged from this wound—a wound I had been carrying since I was fourteen. Even though it was difficult to revisit these memories, I also knew that reopening them would give me a chance to heal them, to be at peace with them, and to have a closer relationship with my mother.

Transitions

"Honey, I have your grandmother here," I said, looking at my client on the computer screen as I spoke. The person on the other side, Kylie, sat still, her expression shifting the moment I mentioned her grandmother's presence. Kylie wasn't the name she was given at birth—it was the name she'd chosen for herself later in life. As soon as I said that her grandmother was with us, I saw something flicker across her face. It wasn't just surprise. It was something deeper. Something that looked an awful lot like sadness.

I abandoned her, the grandmother said to me very quietly. When a Spirit is letting me know that it did something to harm or upset the person that I am reading for, it will speak more softly. I don't believe that the softness is an expression of shame or guilt, since I don't believe that we carry our guilt with us when we depart. But soft and quiet is a message for me to handle this information as delicately as possible.

Those three words hit me right in my stomach: *I abandoned her*. Very seldom do readings activate my emotions, but this one I felt like a tidal wave. The grandmother let me know that not only had she abandoned Kylie, but she'd done so very abruptly, ending their relationship immediately after Kylie shared with her that she was transgender. Kylie had been given a male name at birth, and several years before her grandmother departed from cancer, Kylie had shared with her her most profound truth, only to be abandoned by her family. This felt close to home, as I was at the time working through my own emotions related to my nanan. There was medicine in this session for me, too.

"We were so close. Ever since I can remember, she was my best friend," Kylie told me. "Some kids hang out with other kids, but I hung out with my grandma." Kylie shared a story with me about how they would watch old black-and-white movies together, and her grandma would cook for her while her parents both worked full-time jobs. It reminded me so much of the relationship I had with my nanan.

This is not her fault, Kylie's grandmother said, loudly this time.

"Kylie, she is placing her hands on your shoulders and saying this is not your fault." The grandmother then showed me flowers, a symbol shown to me when there is an anniversary. This day just happened to be Kylie's transition anniversary.

"Kylie, I'm so proud of you for living in your truth, even if this loved one wasn't on board. While I don't know what your journey has been like, I do know how it feels to share who you are with the folks you love and not have it be received the way you had hoped," I told her.

Tell her I was afraid for her, the grandmother said to me and then placed her hands over her chest, letting me know where the cancer was in her body.

"She's letting me know her cancer was in her lungs. You understand this?" I asked Kylie, and she nodded her head, wiping away a small tear. "This might be hard to hear, but she is letting me know that she was afraid for you."

"That was the last thing she said to me . . . that she was afraid how the world would see me and that she couldn't bear to be near me. And then just a few years later, after I transitioned, she passed away from cancer. I never got to see her as . . . as me." Kylie's voice sounded fragile, but I could feel in her energy how strong and incredibly brave she was. All I could think in that moment was that her grandmother knew more about her journey than she realized. In that moment, the grandmother showed me in my mind's eye a stunning yellow dress with flowers all over it. I asked Kylie if she recognized it, and Kylie's face lit up.

"That's the dress I wore to visit Grandma's grave!" And she held up a photo of her wearing the yellow flowered dress, kneeling beside her grandmother's headstone. "I wanted her to *see* me after my transition, and this was the best I could do. I know it's odd to take a photo with a headstone, but I wanted one more photo together. I can't believe you knew that!"

"Kylie, your grandmother showed me that dress as a way to let you know that she not only knows about your transition, but she's also aware that her actions and behaviors are responsible for ending your relationship. You see, honey, the way that Spirit communicates with me is that they not only validate the existence of their energy still in your life, but they also acknowledge their part in your relationship. Your grandmother loves you so much, and she knows that she could have responded differently to you. I never make an excuse for a Spirit, but I'm feeling that she loved you so much, but her fear got in the way. She couldn't get past her fear of how the world would view you, but that isn't your fault or your burden to carry. She wants me to mention a hummingbird tattoo she's showing me. Do you have one?" Kylie then pulled up her sleeve to show me a gorgeous hummingbird tattoo on her arm. Hummingbirds were her grandmother's favorite, she told me, and she got the tattoo in memory of her.

"I've been blaming myself for our relationship ending," Kylie said. "You have no idea how much this has helped me." As she spoke, Kylie's shoulders shifted back, her chin lifted, and light returned to her eyes. The incredible power of her own Spirit began to stir within her, reminding her of who she is. I could see the healing taking place. Her eyes started to sparkle, and there was relief.

How quickly the healing from Spirit can happen when someone is open to receiving it is always a miracle to me. Kylie was ready to let go of the burden of guilt for something that wasn't even her fault. She was ready to release her past because it was becoming too heavy for her to carry. She had transformed her life, and this was the last weight holding her in an old memory. No more hauntings for Kylie.

The Bond I Didn't Realize

We are not our anger, fear, resentment, or past decisions. We are eternal energy forged from love, and what we become here in this human life is the culmination of our actions, thoughts, and behaviors. I believe that at our cores, we are all the purest essence of love, even when our actions align with fear. Fear can take control of our behavior when it gains momentum because fear is sneaky. It tells you that it is keeping you safe, but in reality, it does anything but that. It misleads us and tricks us into thinking our loved ones are our enemies or that we must carry our anger and rage. Because if we don't carry those things from our past, then who are we anyway?

But if we remember that we are love and return to that love, fear has nowhere to hide. Fear cannot exist in the presence of love, much as darkness cannot exist in the presence of light. That doesn't mean we need to run from our fear or disown it or hide from our shadow aspects. In my work with Spirit, I have learned that if we can turn toward our fear and ask, "What can you teach me, and how can I bring love to you in this moment?" we may find that our fear isn't so scary after all.

For a long time, I carried my resentment over how my family handled my coming out as a badge of honor. *They did this horrible thing, and I have every right to feel this way*, I would think to myself. And while that might have been true, the burden of carrying that energy was eating me alive. A few months prior to my nanan passing, I reached out to her to see if, after nearly twelve years since our last interaction, she would be willing to talk. I called her on the phone randomly one afternoon, after she had been on my mind for several days. My finger trembled as I dialed her phone number, unsure if I was making the right decision.

My mother and I had made amends when I was in my mid-twenties. But I hadn't reconnected with my nanan, the person I wanted to reconcile with the most. When she answered the phone, she sounded incredibly surprised that I wanted to see her, but she agreed to see me and offered to cook lunch for us. I was ecstatic, already thinking about the amazing conversations we'd have once we were reunited. I had missed her terribly.

Not ten minutes later, I received a phone call from my mother asking if I'd called Nanan. My mom hadn't been in communication with her family due to their own issues that had surfaced—you see, my mom's parents and some of her siblings weren't the happiest of people. And while I have no doubt that my mom loved her parents, her wounding from them was something she also carried. When they stopped communicating, I wasn't surprised. I was, however, surprised that she knew I had called Nanan.

"You better come home first. There's something you need to see," my mom said to me. When there is something serious happening, my mom has two very different, distinct tones to her voice. The first one is that of anger, when something has really ticked her off and she's ready to get down to business. The other is a calm tone, bordering on kind, even though shit may be hitting the fan. Her tone for this call was the calm voice, which really had me unsettled. My heart started racing, and the ten-minute drive home felt like an eternity. My mom was waiting for me in the kitchen, holding a note from my nanan. It said, "Travis, forget we exist. Do not come over." My nanan hadn't wanted to turn me down on the phone, and instead she'd left a Post-it note on the garage door of my mother's home. These would be the final words I would ever receive from my nanan. A few months later, she crossed over. And for the next decade, I would carry this resentment deep within me, buried away, only to have it eat away at me like a disease.

The week after Kylie's session, it was time to head back to another EMDR appointment to dive back into the wound of my own abandonment. I was ready to see this situation differently. I was ready to begin the journey of letting go.

"What do you notice this time, Travis?" Like watching a movie from a new perspective, this time, I took in the full scene. Yes, my mother was crying, screaming, and visibly shaken, but when I allowed myself to zoom out, I saw something deeper. Beneath the chaos and the raw emotion, I saw fear. But I also saw love. It struck me that despite the way my coming out had been received, my mother's love for me had always been there, pouring out of her, even in its most tangled form. Fear was blocking that love from flowing freely, like a dam holding back a river that was meant to run wild and unhindered.

I saw the same fear in my nanan's face and heard it in the tremor of her voice. I saw it spread to my sister, wrapping around her. Fear had taken control of the room. It had suffocated the chance for love to expand, to create space for understanding and compassion. At that moment, I realized that fear is contagious, and when it has enough momentum, it can control everything and everyone in its path. It moves through people, through generations, shaping the way we respond to the unfamiliar, dictating how we hold or withhold love.

And then, suddenly, I was transported to another memory. One that I hadn't expected—the moment my mother handed me the note from my grandmother. I had been trying to stay grounded in the memory of my coming out, but my mind flashed forward nearly a decade to the weight of that folded piece of paper in my hands. The pain, the rejection. My body felt it all over again. But this time, I was seeing more than just my own pain. I was seeing the chain of pain that had been passed down through my family. And in that moment, I understood: I hadn't just been abandoned by my nanan. My mother had been abandoned by her, too.

Suddenly, this moment was no longer just about me. It was a thread woven into a larger tapestry of generational pain, a story that had been written long before I ever spoke my truth or before I even existed. The resentment and anger I'd carried toward my mother and my grandmother weren't just emotions, they were vibrations of energy that had been traveling all throughout our family. Echoes of fear passed down, again and again.

But in that same realization, something powerful shifted within me. I felt compassion that I hadn't felt before. For the first time, I truly saw my mother, not just as the woman who had struggled with my coming out, but as a daughter who had also longed for acceptance and been denied it. I may never fully understand why my nanan let fear take hold of her, why she chose to close herself off instead of leaning into love. But I could see that my mother, despite everything that had been passed down to her, had made a different choice. She had chosen to move beyond fear. To rebuild. To understand. And in choosing to love, she activated a new vibration. One more kind, more loving. And so damn brave.

That realization changed everything. In that moment, I chose to let go. I forgave her. I forgave her reaction to my coming out. I forgave the fear, the hesitation, the pain. I saw her not as someone who had failed me but as someone who had done her best with what she had, who had decided to move in opposition to the conditioning of her own past. And if she could do that, then so could I.

For so long, I thought I was angry at my mother. I was unable to see past my own pain. But the truth was, there was something deeper than anger. There was also sadness and fear. I was afraid. Afraid of being abandoned again. Afraid that love could be taken away just as quickly as it was given, and sad that our relationship had been tarnished by that fear. But in that moment, I saw that fear no longer had a place in our relationship. My mother had allowed love in, she had allowed herself to be changed and transformed. And now, it was my turn.

After the session, I felt lighter. I decided to take a walk through the quiet streets near my therapist's office, letting the cool air settle into my skin, letting the world around me mirror the clarity I now carried inside. I inhaled deeply, absorbing the scent of the trees, listening to the rhythm of my footsteps. I knew healing was not a single moment but a process. Still, for the first time in years, I felt at peace, knowing that a large part of the anger and grief I had been holding had finally been released.

That day, I made a choice—not only to forgive my mother but to forgive myself. To release the years I had spent clinging to a pain that had become a familiar companion. Sometimes, we hold on to suffering not because we want to, but because it's what we know. It becomes part of our identities, a story we tell ourselves over and over again until we believe it is who we are. But stories can be rewritten. Narratives can change.

I thought of how brave Kylie had been to write herself a new story. I thought of my mother, who had also chosen to rewrite hers. And then, I asked myself: *What will my new story be?*

My new story would be one of forgiveness.

My new story would be that I get to choose how I move forward.

My new story would be that I am open to love.

I would not hold the fear of abandonment so close to my chest, but instead I would hold hope—hope that I will continue to be embraced by my loved ones, by Spirit, by the world itself. But more important, that I would embrace myself.

I now understood that in order to serve others, I had to serve myself first. To heal my wounds. To allow my own transformation. Because healing and forgiveness are not just acts of grace—we must be willing participants in them. Healing means looking at our pain with open eyes and open hearts, without judgment, without resentment, but with the willingness to ask: *What am I ready to let go of? What am I still carrying that no longer serves me?*

It has been said many times that healing is not linear but spiral. That we revisit the same lessons, each time with a deeper understanding. That first dive into healing is often the hardest because it is unfamiliar; we are not used to seeing our wounds so clearly. But the truth is, while our wounds may not be our fault, they are our responsibility. It is up to us to tend to them, to release what is heavy, to choose a life beyond pain.

Forgiveness is not passive or some lovely thought. It is an act of courage. It is standing in the face of old wounds and saying:

I am ready to be free.

As I walked through the streets of Seattle, the sunlight warming my skin, I looked up just in time to see a hummingbird fluttering alongside me. It moved effortlessly, its wings beating fast, yet it appeared suspended in perfect stillness. In that moment, I felt a whisper from beyond, a gentle *thank you* from my nanan. She was free from her physical body and also from her own pain and fear.

I believe that when we depart our physical bodies, we leave our fear behind and return to unconditional love. But we do not have to wait for that freedom. We can experience it here and now. In that moment, I felt sure that Nanan had left behind her fear.

It was a knowing that just as I was free, so was she.

FIVE

Sunshine

Growing up, I didn't have a clear picture of what my life would look like, much less what my purpose was. I always felt there was something within me that I was meant to do, but I had no clue what that thing was. All I knew was that I liked helping others, making people laugh, and connecting with people. Somewhere along the way, I developed this idea that true purpose was reserved for only a lucky few—and how lucky they were to know what that purpose was! I would watch movies where a hero would go on an incredible quest and come out on the other side knowing they had found their purpose. Was purpose something that made you special? And if so, how did the Universe decide who got to be special?

The truth is purpose isn't something that is bestowed upon you or something you have to earn. Purpose is inherent in all of us because our purpose is to live joyfully and create the life we desire.

It isn't a specific role or title but rather a feeling. And when we connect to that feeling, and take action from that place, we feel aligned with a sense of purpose.

This thought sometimes sends our egos into overdrive because the ego tells us we need some fancy title or important job to have purpose and be worthy. That is often the story the world tells us. But, honey, I'm here to tell you—we are worthy simply because we exist.

The search for purpose often becomes something we look for outside ourselves. But I don't believe anything external can give us purpose or meaning. That sense of meaning comes from within—it flows from us. My clients often ask me, "What is my purpose?" And they always look so surprised when I meet their gazes and say, "You're living it right now. Being here is your purpose." That answer can also sound like nails on a chalkboard if you're looking for a more complicated answer. I know it sounded that way to me when I first heard it. However, it isn't believing that our purpose is to simply be who we are that gives us freedom; it's channeling that energy and allowing it to flow that brings us connection and freedom.

The first step to aligning with purpose is to follow what feels satisfying. Spiritual teacher Abraham-Hicks shares that your emotions are your internal GPS, and satisfaction is the clearest sign you're on the right path. What makes you feel alive? When do you lose track of time? What do you love doing, even if no one pays you for it? The answers to those questions will start pointing you toward that alignment. Even when I had no idea what my purpose was, I knew that helping people gave me a feeling beyond description. Every time I felt I'd helped someone, I wanted to keep doing it. Whenever I could make someone laugh, smile, or find peace, I wanted that feeling to multiply.

I worked in the beauty industry for seventeen years, starting as a makeup artist. I felt so deeply connected to that job; doing someone's makeup was so much more than selling them a new eye shadow or foundation. It was about helping them uncover the person they truly felt they were. And makeup had that same effect on me. For the first time in my life, I could express how I felt on the inside. At eighteen, when I was not speaking to my family, makeup became a safe haven for me, a place where I could be bright and sparkly without judgment or shame. With bright eye shadow, lip gloss, and glitter on my face, I felt unstoppable. It was the first time I felt truly seen and embraced for who I was on the inside. And not only was I embraced—I was encouraged to be myself. I was creating a sense of purpose through self-expression.

Eventually, I left makeup artistry and found myself in leadership roles. I discovered a love for helping people define what they wanted in their careers and guiding them to make it happen. Even though I was still in the beauty industry, I became fascinated with spreadsheets, with setting goals for teams and helping those teams reach them. I found a deep sense of identity in leadership and helping people grow. I read books by Brené Brown and Simon Sinek on how to be the best leader I could be, but beyond leadership, these books were teaching me how to connect with an inherent energy that had always existed within me, just like in my journey with mediumship.

The very first time I coached a sales team in cosmetics to reach a team goal and saw their eyes light up with excitement for our collective win, I felt a deep sense of pride. It was a feeling of joy rushing through my body, and I knew it was about more than just sales. It was about connecting a team and helping them feel inspired by their own efforts. If you had asked me then if that was my purpose, I would have said, "Absolutely."

Both these chapters in my life felt purposeful because, even though I didn't fully realize it at the time, I was connecting to an energy within me and channeling it to help others. When I started giving private readings for clients, something shifted. Before, my sense of purpose came from watching others be satisfied with the work I delivered. Whether it was someone liking how I did their makeup or my boss praising me for hitting a sales goal, my sense of worth was tied to how others felt about my performance.

In working with Spirit, none of it is about me. In fact, the less it is about me, the easier the messages flow. Otherwise, I try to add my own interpretation, and the messages become clunky. It's a bit of a paradox. The work with Spirit isn't about me, yet it requires me to show up as my full self. That doesn't mean I have to be healed or be some ascended master who has given up all earthly possessions. It does mean that I can't hide from myself. No matter how hard it might be, I have to face my life and show up for myself, and the Universe/Spirit shows up in kind. In other words, my own healing has to happen in order for me to help others. There's a proverb that says, "Healer, heal thyself," and I have found this to be a gentle reminder whenever I try to avoid doing my own inner work.

After leaving my long career in the beauty industry, I forgot what my purpose was. It was September 2020, and I was newly sober from alcohol. For years, I had been hiding behind an identity of overworking. I was shedding the layers of who I no longer was, but there was one small hiccup—I'd forgotten who I really was.

For several years, I'd been focused on chasing job promotions and title changes. Those titles became my identity. I was leading teams with great success, but most of the time, I lived in fear that I wasn't doing enough to keep my bosses satisfied. I kept pushing myself to perform, and in doing so, I had drifted far from what I truly enjoyed—helping others and feeling connected. The day my position was terminated, I felt relief. Deep down, I knew this was the Universe guiding me toward what was next.

The days floated by, and I thought that surely, by some miracle, the Universe was going to knock on my door with my new job title, and I would skip off into the sunset and live happily ever after. That didn't happen. But what did happen was still a miracle.

For years, I'd been giving readings to friends with tarot cards and connecting with souls who had passed, but I never shared that part of me publicly. It was something I did at parties after people had had a few drinks, when it felt more socially acceptable. One night, I got on TikTok and went live. A follower asked me for something to cheer them up. At the time, I'd been posting videos in which I applied my nighttime skin-care routine while delivering inspirational messages before bed. That night, I decided to grab my tarot deck instead.

I began shuffling, intuitively choosing cards, and delivering messages based on what I felt and sensed. More people started asking for readings, and then more, and more. Before I knew it, the livestream had more than fifteen hundred people watching. It was the feeling of being seen all over again, except this time, it wasn't coming from something external. It was coming from an energy flowing through me that I was sharing with the intention of helping others. In that moment, I knew this was the beginning of a new path forward.

Love That Knows No Bounds

Several weeks and lots of studying about mediumship later, I found myself giving a reading to a woman whose son had left this earth by his own choosing. He was seventeen years old and had decided he could no longer remain in this lifetime. This was the first time I had ever connected to someone in the spirit world who had passed by suicide.

When I sat down with his mother, I knew this was going to be a different kind of reading. I didn't know how he had passed before the session began, but I could feel that his was a departure unlike any I had encountered before. Up until this point, most of my sessions had focused on life direction, career decisions, or receiving messages from grandparents or father figures. As I tuned in to the energy, I felt a heaviness in my chest. It wasn't necessarily an apology but, rather, an acknowledgment that this soul had left by his own choice. I described to his mother how her son had passed, details about his two siblings, and some of the tattoos he had on his body.

Although I stayed professional, in my mind, I was freaking out. How in the hell did I know all of this? It wasn't a feeling—it was a knowing. It was as if I had known this soul before, and he was reminding me of things I knew about him. Was I the right person to deliver this kind of message? And if so, why me?

Tell Mom I see her sniffing my band T-shirt, he said to me. In my mind, I thought, *Seriously?* And then he said, *Seriously.*

When I hear Spirit, I do not hear a literal voice. It comes in as a high-pitched ringing or pressure in my ear, and then my brain translates that frequency into thoughts and words. Sometimes what comes through can sound a little ridiculous, and it makes me go, "Are you *sure*?" to the Spirit. But hey, it's my job to deliver the mail, not to read it.

"Honey, he wants me to talk about you smelling his old band T-shirt. Do you know what this means?" I hoped she understood, or this would be super awkward. She immediately covered her mouth and began crying. Earlier that morning, she told me, she had been sitting in his bedroom, holding on to the T-shirt of the band he was in and was breathing into it. The shirt still smelled like him—he'd departed from this Earth only two months prior to our session. The Spirit of those who have departed will show me things that might seem insignificant but actually mean so much. They show the daily activities of those they love because they want them to know that they are with them in every moment, especially the difficult ones.

"He was my purpose." She choked out those words, her body nearly crumbling in the chair she was sitting in. As a person with zero children, I fully admit that I will never know the pain of a child departing this Earth, and I never pretend that I do. What I do know is that as I sat with this client, her despair was palpable. What I also know is that, since this reading, I have connected hundreds of parents to the souls of their departed children, and I still don't have the words to describe exactly how dense the energy of that grief is.

I believe that love is fluid. I believe it can take many forms, many depths, and ultimately that love is what connects us all. I also believe that grief works in the same way—it can take many forms and many depths. Our grief is proportionate to the love we have for our departed. In that moment, the only thing that could come out of my mouth to this beautiful soul's mother was "How lucky is he to have someone who loves him so deeply and for him to know how much you love him?"

"Is he . . . you know . . . in . . . in a bad place?" she asked. I took a deep breath and took my time to receive the answer to this question.

No, I heard him say. *It's not like that.* And suddenly my body was filled with a rush of energy. I felt knowings I had never understood before about what happens when we depart this Earth. I've never believed that when someone ends their life it's a straight shot to a lower-vibrational plane. Spirit has shown me time and time again, just like in this session, that the soul still returns to high-frequency love, and there is no punishment for those who depart from suicide.

"He's not in a lower-vibrational plane. He's returned to the essence that is high-vibrational love. Love that is connected to Oneness. Love that can't be described with words, just feelings." And as I shared what this was like, her son showed me that souls continue to expand once we depart this physical vessel. That our purpose as energy is to continue expanding. This isn't to be confused with productivity or doing but rather with being. Being love and allowing that love to expand.

"He was my purpose," she repeated. "I just don't know what I'm going to do."

When I couldn't find the right words, I asked her son in Spirit: "Give me the words to serve."

You are my sunshine, I heard her son say to me, a gentle tune in my ear. I repeated the words back to her, and she rolled up her sleeve. After her son had transitioned, she'd had that phrase tattooed on her wrist, along with a sunflower. It was the song she sang to him, even as he became a young adult. She shared that she had been humming it to herself all morning, and it provided comfort to her when the grief of her son's passing became too unbearable.

"May I offer some words?" I asked her, wanting to be sensitive about the information that I shared with her.

"Of course." She wiped tears away with a tissue.

"I understand that your son and your other children are your purpose. But what if that purpose isn't gone—just the physical vessel that represented him?"

"I don't follow," she said.

"Well, do you still love him?"

"Of course!" she said as she sat up and looked at me with intent.

"Of course you do! Your grief is proof of that. Grief reminds us of the deep love that we carry. What if that love for him *is* the purpose? The purpose isn't something grand; it's something we do with intention. Can you intend to continue to love him and allow that to be purposeful? And can you continue to pour that love into other areas of your life?"

She smiled at me, nodded, and said, "I can't explain it, but I feel lighter." And in that moment, I knew her son had given me exactly what she needed to hear.

As we closed the session, her son offered one final message for his mother: *Become a nurse.* In that instant, I watched his soul gently touch her shoulder, a gesture so tender it brought a stillness to the room.

"Your son is showing me that nursing might be the path for you," I said.

The woman's eyes welled up, and a soft smile spread across her face. She reached into her bag and pulled out a pamphlet for a local nursing program. "He would say that," she said, holding it up like a confirmation from the Universe. "I've been thinking about going back. I left nursing school when I got pregnant with him, but lately . . . it's been on my heart again."

When she spoke, I felt something shift—an unmistakable clarity that filled the space between us. As we wrapped up the session, I realized I had experienced something profound. For the first time in my journey as a medium, I felt completely aligned, not because of validation or praise, but because I had witnessed healing flow in its purest form. The feeling was unlike anything I'd known before, and I wanted to etch it into my memory. Closing my eyes, I silently thanked her son's soul—not just for the clarity he'd brought to her, but for the clarity he had gifted me, as well.

SUNSHINE

Healing with Purpose

Our purpose and our healing are often intertwined, and as we heal, our next steps become clearer. The wounds we carry often lead us to the very things we are meant to share with the world. Our deepest pain can become the doorways to our greatest calling. The challenges we've faced—the heartbreaks, the setbacks, the losses—are not meaningless. They are invitations to transform, to expand, and to bring light to others who may be walking a similar path.

Healing and purpose are intertwined because healing awakens us to the love and joy within us. Healing isn't so you never have to experience the pain of the past, it's so you can allow yourself to move forward despite the past. When we begin to heal, we start seeing ourselves and the world differently. We recognize patterns that have held us back, we release limiting beliefs, and we begin to reconnect with the core of who we are. That reconnection often reignites old dreams, forgotten passions, and soul callings that had been buried beneath years of conditioning and pain.

One of the greatest myths about purpose is that we have to be completely healed before we can step into it. Many people delay their calling because they feel they aren't ready yet. They believe they need to reach some perfected state of being before they can serve others or make a meaningful impact. But the truth is healing is a continual process. If we waited until we were fully healed, we would never begin. We are always in a state of becoming, and we never fully arrive because we never truly end. It's infinite, and it's beautiful. The sentiment that we are never done used to be daunting to me. Now, I find freedom in it because there's always an opportunity to do something different from what's been done before. Our own Universe is still expanding, and we are a reflection of that energy. The Universe isn't done, and neither are we.

The most powerful purpose-driven work comes from those who are still in process, still learning, still growing, and still evolving. People don't need perfection. They need authenticity. They need someone who understands, someone who has been there, someone who can say, "I see you. I've sat with my own discomfort. I've sat with my own shadows and have brought love to them. And you are not alone."

Your healing can shape your purpose in ways you never imagined. Maybe the grief you have experienced allows you to hold space for others in their sorrow. Maybe the self-doubt you've battled inspires you to empower others to believe in themselves. Maybe the struggles you've overcome become the road map that helps others find their ways.

If you are currently in a season of healing, trust that it is guiding you somewhere meaningful. The pieces that feel broken now may one day become the very foundation of your purpose. Sometimes, we need to break apart so we can come together more holistically. Instead of asking, "Why did this happen to me?" try asking, "How can this experience shape me? How can I use what I have learned to serve others?" And then watch your life change right in front of your eyes. Healing and purpose walk hand in hand. One fuels the other. As you heal, your purpose becomes more apparent. As you live your purpose, your healing deepens. And through it all, you are becoming exactly who you were meant to be.

A Signier Sign

Later that day, as I wandered through an antique shop, my thoughts drifted back to my client's story and the way her son's love had nudged her toward rediscovering her path. As I traced my fingers over the worn edges of a gilded picture frame, a thought settled into my heart: Our purpose isn't a destination. It's a living, breathing essence that evolves with us. For me, the mediumship work had shifted the form of my purpose, but its core—helping others—remained constant. The same was true for the mother I'd met earlier. Her purpose wasn't gone or lost; it was simply waiting to be rediscovered, polished like the treasures in the shop around me. Her purpose was love. Pure, radiant love. And through her son's guidance, she was reminded to channel it in a way that served others.

The same is true for all of us. No matter how our lives twist and turn, the essence of who we are and what we're here to do stays steady. It's our job to listen, to lean in, and to trust the gentle nudges along the way. Listen to your intuition. Your purpose isn't something your mind has to figure out. It's something your soul already knows. Those little nudges, gut feelings, and recurring ideas are not random. They are whispers from the Universe guiding you back to yourself.

I walked up and down the aisles, admiring items made of beautiful glass and wood, expertly crafted to be something useful or beautiful or both. And there, among the treasures of the antique store, was a beautiful print of a sun with the phrase YOU ARE MY

SUNSHINE in bold text. I held the print in my hands, in awe of the synchronicity of the moment, my body buzzing with the rush of connection and joy.

"Thank you," I said quietly, close to a whisper. *Thank you*, I heard back. That day I was surer than ever that I was on the path I was meant to walk. Every decision, every choice, every conscious step forward had led me to where I was, and for the first time in my life I felt grateful to be exactly where I was standing.

Spirit wasn't asking me to be perfect or fully healed. All that was required of me was that I tap into my deeper knowing and show up for myself. My purpose wasn't a job title; it was a state of being. If I could allow myself to share this beautiful ability of connection to Spirit authentically while also showing up for myself, then that would be enough. While healing others while taking care of myself would prove to be a balancing act, I knew that I was even more ready to dive into being of service to others through my connection to Spirit.

I noticed something else in the antique shop that day, which felt so small but also so big. For the first time in as long as I could remember, I felt relaxed and secure. I could breathe into my body and feel completely safe. Not only did I think I was right where I was supposed to be, I felt it, too. It would continue to be a journey of reminding myself to slow down and be in the moment, but for now, I could catch my breath. And in that moment, breathing became my purpose.

SIX

Change

Change can shake things up, whether we ask for it or not. Sometimes, it comes as an exciting new opportunity, a fresh start, or a long-awaited shift. Other times, it arrives in ways we didn't expect, asking us to release what we thought was certain. No matter how it appears, change always brings an invitation: to grow, expand, and step into something new.

But let's be honest—change can feel uncomfortable. Even when we know it's for the best, there's often a sense of loss that comes with it. When we move forward, we are also leaving something behind, and that can stir up emotions we were not expecting. There is a kind of grief in letting go, not because we are losing parts of ourselves, but because we are stepping into the unknown.

The mind loves certainty. It craves routine, predictability, and solid ground. But life does not work that way. Life moves. It evolves. It calls us forward in ways we could never fully plan for. The more we resist change, the harder it feels. But when we lean into it and allow ourselves to be present with whatever is unfolding, we open ourselves to something greater than what we could have imagined.

I have learned that change does not always come with a road map. Sometimes, it requires trust before clarity. It asks us to walk forward without knowing exactly where the path leads. And even when it feels like everything is shifting beneath our feet, there is always something steady within us—our ability to adapt, create, and find meaning in the transitions.

Oh, Brother

Tara had come to me for a mediumship reading, but we ended up diving into her personal life and the current energy she was sitting in.

We began the session by connecting with her brother, who had been in a fatal car accident seventeen years earlier. Several years older than she was, he had lived with severe depression when he was in his physical body. A loving, kind, and warm spirit, her brother began the session by making a joke about her new hairstyle.

"He always teased me about my hair," she said, smiling. "I have big curly hair that's always been long, and recently, I decided to cut it all off. It's funny because as I was getting my hair cut, I actually said to my stylist that my brother would laugh at how short I wanted it."

"Well, for the record, I love your hairstyle," I said with a smile.

Tell her that everything with the job is going to be okay, her brother said to me.

"He wants me to let you know that everything is going to be okay as it relates to your job. He's showing me a closed door. Does that make sense to you? He's making me feel like you just left your job."

Tara's eyes began to redden and fill with tears. She let me know that her role of seventeen years was no more; her company had needed to downsize to save money. I learned during the reading that she had begun the job around the time that her brother had passed.

"Travis, I don't know what to do," she said. I could feel the worry and doubt radiating from her.

She hated the job, her brother said to me. Something that felt almost like relief for her passed through me.

"Don't shoot the messenger," I said, "but your brother is telling me that you hated the job." I looked at Tara with deep compassion, as I have been in the same situation myself.

"Oh, that job was fucking awful!" she said, blending laughter and tears.

She told me that she'd worked excessively long hours and that her boss didn't appreciate her. Every couple of weeks she'd found herself in her boss's office sharing her frustrations that nothing had changed to make things better for her. Tara was frustrated, and while she was devastated about the job ending, she shared that she also felt relief.

"Is it weird that even though I'm so incredibly stressed about what I'm going to do now, I've slept better the last few nights than I've slept in over two years?"

"Honey, I'm not surprised to hear that at all."

Tell her that it's time to follow her dream of becoming a photographer. Her brother then showed me an older camera in my mind's eye.

"Your bother is making me feel like there's a bigger dream that you have for yourself. Do you want to be a photographer? He keeps showing me an old camera."

Her eyes lit up, and again I saw myself in her. It was the same look I'd had on my face when Teri, the medium I'd first gone to see, had told me I'd be giving readings one day. It was a look that said, "You see me. You really see me."

"I love taking photographs! That old camera he's showing you is probably the one our dad got me when I was younger. I still have it!"

She's been asking for a nudge forward! This is it.

"Tara, listen, I know how scary it can be to take a huge leap, especially when you don't feel like you had much of a say in the matter. But what your brother keeps making me feel is that it was time for a change. What I believe to be true is that when we are ready to fly, the Universe will help nudge us forward. At first, it's a tapping on the shoulder. When we ignore that, it becomes a shove. And when we ignore the shove, we get thrown out of the nest."

I could tell that my words were resonating with Tara. She kept nodding her head and smiling, as if she finally understood why things were unfolding the way they were.

Surrender

Our souls are not here for the comfort of our egos. When we have a desire within us, whether it's to be a photographer, a teacher, a dancer, a spiritual healer, a writer, you name it, the Universe will conspire to help us align with that path. Sometimes, that means that our souls will lead us to lessons we need to learn to make the necessary adjustments to grow. Most of the time it isn't comfortable, but uncomfortable doesn't have to equal miserable.

Our egos, or the parts of ourselves that hold fear, do not like being uncomfortable or uncertain. Our souls, however, do not care about uncertainty or discomfort because our souls grow and expand in the face of uncertainty and pain. Our souls know that we are always safe and divinely guided. Our souls embrace change, while our egos avoid it like cats to bathwater. But our egos aren't trying to keep us from growth; rather, they are only trying to keep us safe. And often, the safe path that looks more appealing can be the path of delaying the inevitable.

While I believe we can take multiple paths in life, those paths fall under two categories. The first is the path that might take longer but has a gentler unfolding. The other, while it's faster, often feels like the equivalent of ripping off a Band-Aid. Most people choose the longer, paved path because it's more comfortable. But sometimes, the desires within us are so strong that our souls can't help but take the path that is paved. That's what was happening to Tara, and I have been in that situation many times myself.

My work with Spirit has led me to believe we all have a greater purpose, and change is a big part of uncovering it. If we are avoiding change, the Universe will conspire and consort to help us let go of what is holding us back. Letting go is not about losing. It's about making space. It's about trusting that when something leaves your life—whether it's a job, a relationship, or an old version of you—it is because something better is waiting to take its place.

The Universe is always guiding us, always working behind the scenes to clear the path ahead. But sometimes, we hold on too tightly to what is familiar, afraid that we will be left with nothing if we release our grip. But letting go is not an emptying. It is an opening. It is an act of faith that says, "I trust that what is meant for me will find me, and I do not have to cling to what no longer aligns."

There is a kind of beauty in surrender, in realizing that we do not have to carry everything with us. We give ourselves permission to release old fears, limiting beliefs, and the weight of what no longer serves us. When we do, we create space for clarity, peace, and something new and unexpected to enter our lives. It's worth remembering that what the Universe can deliver will always be better than what we could have imagined for ourselves.

Surrender might sound beautiful in theory, but it feels terrifying in practice. For the longest time, I thought surrender meant giving up, as if letting go of control meant I was failing in some way. But what I've learned is that surrender isn't about quitting—it's about trust. It's about recognizing that we don't have to force or micromanage every detail of our lives for things to work out.

Surrender and change go hand in hand. Every time I've resisted change, clinging to what felt familiar, I've made the process harder for myself. But the moment I allowed myself to trust—really trust—that the Universe was guiding me somewhere meaningful, things started falling into place in ways I never could have orchestrated on my own.

Tapping into the energy of Spirit and receiving messages from those who have departed require my full surrender. I must surrender my doubt, fear, ego, and judgment and allow love to be fully present. One day, I realized I didn't need to give readings in order to surrender those things and allow love to take the lead. When I need to remind myself of this, I repeat the affirmation "I allow myself to trust love completely." This helps me remember that there is no need to force anything in my life. Surrender means I can stop pushing and rushing and be open to possibility.

But surrender doesn't mean sitting back and doing nothing. It means showing up in full faith and doing your part and then releasing the need to control how or when things unfold. Sometimes it's showing up and saying to the Universe or God, "I have no idea what I'm doing. Guide me and I will take the first step." When we meet the Universe with aligned action, we in turn receive an energetic turbo boost. Often, that inspired action is letting go of what we are holding on to out of fear. It's understanding that uncertainty is where the real magic is. If there is a lack of certainty, there is necessarily an abundance of possibility.

The Universe does not ask us to let go without giving us something in return. It brings signs, synchronicities, and small nudges that remind us we are supported. When we listen and trust, we begin to see that every ending carries the seed of a beginning. Like a farmer or a gardener, we must tend to the conditions so that the seeds can grow. That's our only job. We cannot control what grows from the ground. That's above our pay grade. But we can tend the soil and receive the magic that is ready for us when the time is right.

Letting go is also not about giving up. It's about giving ourselves the gift of freedom. It's about believing that life is unfolding exactly as it should and that, when we release with love, we make room for something even greater to arrive.

"So what do I do now?" Tara asked. "I feel aligned with everything you're saying, but now what?"

She has some things already started! her brother shared. He sounded excited.

"Your brother is telling on you just a bit. He says you've already started something?"

Tara looked amazed. She shared with me that, just months earlier, she'd created an LLC for her photography business. She said that she didn't know why she was starting it because she didn't have any actual business, but it just felt right. I think that happens with us. Sometimes, the Universe nudges us to begin something, whether it's an LLC, researching topics that are of interest to us, or getting us mentally, physically, and energetically prepared to make a shift.

When I started my own LLC, Warrior Unicorn, in April 2020, before I began giving readings professionally, I was standing in the grocery store and out of nowhere felt a nudge to start an LLC. I had no idea why—it just felt like a necessary step. At the time, I envisioned something completely different from what I'm doing now. Less than a year later, I would be giving readings professionally.

This was what had happened with Tara. She'd received the knowing or the feeling that she should start an LLC even though she didn't quite know how or when it would come in handy. And now her brother made me feel that she was on the brink of something truly incredible. All Tara needed was a slight nudge forward, or in this case a shove. Again, that's how the Universe can be sometimes. When we're too afraid or hesitant to take a leap forward but we deeply desire it, the Universe will always nudge or shove us forward.

Tell her that she is brave. And then he showed me the word in script.

"Honey, your brother is reminding you of how brave you are," I said. "Maybe you should have it tattooed on you!" I joked. I paused as she wiped another tear from her eye and then began rolling up her sleeve.

"I have *brave* tattooed on my wrist," she said, holding out her arm to show me the word BRAVE in bold letters. Spirit never ceases to amaze me with the evidence of their continuation beyond a physical body. I love how Spirit shares the things that have happened after they transitioned, like tattoos or memories that took place after their passing. But what I find even more remarkable is how meaningful these things are to the people I have been called to help. It provides them with reassurance that our loved ones are still with us, that they're still watching over us, and that they are still very much intrinsically connected in our lives. Since Tara's brother has a higher perspective of her life, I asked him for some advice for her on how she could easily transition through this change.

Tell her to remember to be honest with herself and what she wants.

"Your brother wants you to be honest about what you truly want," I told her.

I could sense psychically that something in her energy field was blocking her from moving forward with her desire to be a photographer. I'm not a therapist, but I know when a mental block is holding someone back. For me, it feels like a dense energy sitting right in the head and heart space. As I leaned into it, I could immediately recognize the feeling. It was doubt.

Doubt has a weight to it, a density that lingers. When I tap into that energy, I can feel it like a fog—uncertainty, hesitation, the kind of confusion that makes everything feel just out of reach. It's a feeling I know all too well, one that can keep even the strongest dreams at a standstill.

But there's something else that's potent about doubt. It can, if we allow it, reinforce our faith. Doubt can shake us or it can strengthen us, or both. In moments of doubt, we can dissect our beliefs, and in the process, we can discover the strength we forgot we had. Doubt can be a gift because it can make us question ourselves to the point of remembering why we think or feel the way we do in the first place. It can also gift us new beliefs after we reevaluate what we've been clinging to.

"Honey, who gave you this story of doubt around being a photographer?"

More tears. Tara explained that although her father meant well, he had told her there was no way she could make money working for herself as a photographer. Her father had been a successful man in finance, and he believed in working hard toward something—whether you loved it or not—in order to make money. In turn, Tara adopted this philosophy and found herself in a job she didn't love, working exceptionally hard to make money in a job that didn't feel aligned with her. She described her father as strict, as someone who deeply valued an honest day's work. Tara believed in honest work, as well, but she also believed there was another way to achieve it. And she was right.

Often, we pick up the stories our parents tell us and adopt them as our own. We might grow up watching a parent work tirelessly at something they don't really love, and as children, we absorb that. We begin to believe that this must be our path, too. Creative careers are rarely encouraged, and if they are, they often come with a story or the misunderstanding that you can't make enough money doing them.

The day I finally left the beauty industry, I called my mom and told her I was going to be a full-time medium. Her first question was "What kind of health insurance benefits does that come with? And is there a 401(k)?"

I smiled and said, "I'm sure the HR department for Spirit will reach out to me shortly and let me know about their benefits package."

Now, this isn't to say all parents are like this. I know plenty of parents with creative professions who share the joy and magic of their work with their children. But I often meet people who feel stuck, who have a deep desire to tap into the more spiritual or creative aspects of themselves and live a life that feels more purposeful, but they aren't sure how to begin.

That's the gift of change—especially when we don't set that change into motion ourselves. Change causes us to question who we are, what we believe in, and what we feel most aligned with.

When we go through times of great transition and uncertainty starts to creep in, that is our opportunity to really look at where our wounds are. Who told us that change was something to fear? Where did we learn that stepping into something new had to come with resistance? And how can we rewire or reprogram that belief so that change feels like an invitation rather than a threat?

Change can be one of our greatest blessings because it reflects back to us the parts of ourselves that are ready to grow. It tells us, "Hey, there's a part of you that is holding on tightly to what is familiar, but if you can lean into this moment, you'll discover an even deeper version of who you are." It asks us to bring light to the places within us that feel uncertain and trust that we are capable of navigating what comes next.

On the surface, my client Tara was facing a career change, but it was so much deeper than that. Isn't that how change works? We think we're just making a shift in one area of our lives, but it ripples out into everything. What looks like a simple career transition on the outside can feel like a complete identity shift on the inside. We find ourselves questioning who we are, what we truly want, and whether we are ready to take up more space in the world.

Yes, there are psychological explanations for why our minds resist the unknown, but there are also spiritual and energetic reasons that change feels so uncomfortable. We feel resistance because we know, at a soul level, that change calls us deeper. It asks us to step into the full expression of who we are, just a little more. It's not just about the new job, the new city, the new relationship, or whatever shifts we face—it's about stepping into greater, more expanded versions of ourselves. And that is where the magic happens.

The defining moments in change don't come from the change itself, but from what we decide to do with it. As things shift in our lives, we have a choice to make. We can keep choosing the same thing, even though the change keeps happening and requires us to feel discomfort every time, or we can lean into the unknown, surrender to the Universe, and allow ourselves to go with the flow of transformation.

In this particular case, the Universe was allowing Tara to choose a different path, one that felt less certain but more aligned with who she was—a creator who wanted to share beauty through the lens of her camera. We ended our session, and I gave her some homework. Her assignment was to script out how she wanted to feel once she was fully living as a photographer and how she would nurture herself when she inevitably hit hurdles along her path to more freedom. For that's what change is—an opportunity to be free.

We avoid change for various reasons. Sometimes it's because uncertainty is uncomfortable. Sometimes it's because, deep down, we don't feel deserving of what we have been asking for. And sometimes, it's a very special blend of both. Our job isn't to judge ourselves for feeling uncertain during times of change. It's to show up for the parts of us that carry that fear and continue moving forward. No matter where the story comes from, the work is the same—be there for the aspects of yourself that need you. When we can sit with that uncertainty and ask, "What are you here to help me see?" we unlock aspects of ourselves we didn't even realize needed to be free.

We are never alone in change. Our team in Spirit is always supporting us, guiding us, and reminding us that transformation isn't something to fear—it's something to embrace. When we start seeing change the way Spirit does—as inevitable, as part of the flow of existence—we unlock a new level of freedom.

After all, Spirit has already experienced one of the greatest shifts of all. They went from being physical beings to nonphysical, moving from one form of existence to another with complete trust. And if they can make *that* transition *and* continue to love, guide, and communicate with us, then maybe the changes we face here in our earthly bodies aren't as daunting as they seem. From their perspective, change isn't an ending. It's an expansion and a natural process. And when we begin to view it that way, too, our potential becomes unlimited.

SEVEN

Socks

S pirit has a way of letting me know that it's time to connect, even before a client joins the reading. Midafternoon light poured into my office as I sat waiting for my client to appear in our Zoom session. Prior to starting a reading, I always get this feeling in my gut akin to nerves. What I've learned over the years is that it isn't nerves at all, but the energy of loved ones and Spirit telling me they are ready to communicate. This energy radiates throughout my solar plexus (the energy center above the navel, below the center of the chest) like a buzzing that moves all through my body. Over the years, I learned to lean into the feelings instead of pushing against them, and it's allowed me to tap into a world of potential within me that I didn't know existed.

As the reading time approached, I gently leaned into the energy around me. Even though I never know who my clients are hoping will come through, I usually have a good idea before we even begin. The strong presence of a male came to the forefront, as if he'd been patiently waiting on me. His energy felt extremely kind and gentle, and I knew, without a doubt, that this was someone's husband.

Kathy arrived right on time for her session, and before I could even say hello, she said, "Oh my God, I'm so nervous."

"It's okay," I said. "I get nervous before readings, too, sometimes."

Kathy had never met a medium before, much less had a reading, and her loving husband immediately made me aware that she was still in the depths of grief. Spirit communicates with me through my own seeing, hearing, and feeling, and I could sense the deep, heavy grief that she carried in her body. I also sensed that she had her guard up.

"Kathy, here's what your loved one is sharing with me," I began, going over the details about the man who had come to sit with us for the afternoon. He told me he'd passed earlier than expected from a rare form of cancer. He provided information about their children and grandchildren and told me that the day of this reading also happened to be their wedding anniversary. Kathy's body language softened the more I showed her I was connected to her loving husband. She began to cry, which can be a pretty common occurrence.

"I feel as though he's here with us right now," she said. "It's been so difficult without him. While Bob was sick, I was his caretaker, and all my time and focus had been on him. Throughout our marriage, I focused on looking after the children. Most of my life has been dedicated to taking care of him and our kids. He worked so hard to support our family, and I felt it was my duty to ensure that he was taken care of until the very end."

"He says you married very young."

This made Kathy smile.

She's thinking about the time we first met. I tripped right in front of her when I went to say hello, her husband said to me.

"Bob is telling me about the time that you first met. It sounds like quite the story. What's all this about him tripping?"

Kathy's eyes lit up, and she stopped crying. She started recounting the story of how their relationship began. Our time together continued with more stories about Bob, his passing, and how Kathy had been spending her days since he had departed from his physical body.

"What I'm unsure of . . ." Her voice began to shake, and tears welled up in her eyes as the brief moment of joy she'd felt began to fade. "I'm unsure of how to move forward."

This is always the challenging part about my work because, no matter what I say, no matter how real the connection to their loved one feels, I can't bring them back into their physical body for my client. All I can do is continue delivering messages. You see, when I'm delivering these messages from Spirit, I'm not in a place of empathy. I do feel compassion for the person who's right in front of me, but I'm also deeply aware that our loved ones, even though they are no longer in physical bodies, do not leave us. Leaving our physical bodies just means that we're now operating at a higher frequency. As a medium, I'm like a radio. I gently tune myself to the frequency of people's loved ones. I'm the messenger, the conduit between them and their loved one.

Sir, I asked in my head, *What would you like me to say to your wife?*

Tell her that I love her. And tell her that it's time she finds a way to take care of herself.

"Kathy, your husband is making me feel like you need to take care of yourself. Do you understand what this means?"

"I do." She nodded as she wiped tears from her face. "Since he's been gone, I've been volunteering my time at our church and helping my kids take care of their children."

"That sounds really lovely," I said.

"Yeah, whenever I'm sad, I volunteer my time, or I do something kind for someone else. As you can imagine, I've been volunteering a lot of my time lately." She chuckled and smiled.

Tell her that Bob said to let someone take care of her for a change.

"Honey, Bob is saying that it's time you let someone take care of you."

"I know. Plenty of folks have offered, I just feel bad accepting their help."

"Well, how about this, Kathy? I believe that whatever we put out into the Universe, the Universe finds a way of giving it back to us. But we have to be willing to receive it. How about you tell the Universe that you're ready to receive some help?"

Kathy smiled at me. Her shoulders relaxed as she let out a deep breath. I could practically see the tension leaving her body. She had a softness to her that she hadn't had when we'd begun our session together, and it was beautiful to witness. I'm never privy to what's going on in someone's head when we have a session together. What I know for sure about mediumship and how Spirit works is that, while we're in session, healing energy is being delivered to the person I'm reading for. Truthfully, I think that container for self-healing can happen even when we just show up for each other. As a medium, I'm simply holding space for energy to flow—I'm not the one that's carrying out the actual healing. The person I'm reading for is doing their own healing.

In that moment, I knew that Kathy was able to acknowledge the suffering within herself in a way she hadn't before. Between the sheer weight and thickness of her grief and her innate need to help others, she was ignoring a vital part of herself that desired to be witnessed. The part of her that was saying, "I'm hurting, and I don't want to hurt alone."

Kathy peered down at her hands as she opened up, verbalizing what she already knew but feeling more open to admitting it now that her husband had called it out. "I guess the way forward is to let people help me when they offer to help."

"That does seem like it would make things a little bit easier for you, don't you think?"

"I think it sounds lovely. Thank you, Bob."

Sometimes, we know deep down what we really need, but for many, like Kathy, we require a little push from our loved ones to help us accept it and take action.

Kathy and I concluded our session, and I took some time to release the energy from our time together. It's important for me to do so after a session because otherwise someone else's energy will stick with me. I love people so much, and I find that if I don't release the reading, I'll be thinking about the folks that I've read for for days, wondering how they're doing or if they've been able to move forward. It can get in the way of other sessions. Still, while I need to let go of the specific intricacies and connection of each reading, I do find that some of the overall messages stick with me—usually the ones that contain lessons I also need to learn. And in this case, that was absolutely true.

Rejection, Some Candles, and a Lesson

"I'm sorry, Travis; I think you're great, but I'm just not ready for a relationship."

This was the fifth text message I'd received like this in the span of a few months. I had decided to try dating again—it had been almost two years since my last relationship, and I was ready to dive back in and open my heart to someone. But it was the same story with every person I met. The first date was wonderful, but by the second, they'd decided they weren't ready for what I was looking for. Normally, when someone tells me that they aren't ready for a relationship, I take it in stride and chalk it up to the Universe looking out for me. But for some reason, this text message struck deep.

"What is wrong with me?" I asked myself, sitting alone in the kitchen as I read the words over and over again.

"I think you're great, but I'm just not ready for a relationship."

I took a deep breath and heard a voice clearly in my head say, *What part of you isn't available to be loved and cared for?*

This was the voice of one of my Spirit Guides. As you can imagine, I was incredibly annoyed by this very resonant question. Deep down, I knew that I was neglecting a part of myself that was hurting and needed to be witnessed. As I pondered that truth, Kathy's voice echoed through my head: "Whenever I'm sad, I volunteer my time, or I do something kind for someone else."

I had errands to run, so I said out loud to the Universe, "Put someone on my path today that I can help."

I always trust the Universe to show up, even when I'm not sure how it will reveal itself. How the Universe shows up is none of my business. We can get in the way of major blessings when we try to micromanage the Universe. Plus, the Universe always delivers above and beyond what I could ever dream up for myself. My only job is to receive. On this particular December day, my errands led me to a local Target. As I pulled into the parking lot, I noticed a gentleman sitting nearby with a tattered sign written in patchy ink. It read: "Homeless. Hungry. Please help."

I laughed at the Universe's sense of humor. I'd asked for a sign that morning, and here it was right in front of me. A *literal* sign that couldn't be ignored.

I parked my car and walked into the Target. As I grabbed a shopping basket, I wondered what this individual might need. I perused the aisles, looking for things I thought could be helpful. I picked up protein bars, bottles of water, hygienic wipes, and other things that I hoped would make this person's day a little easier. Even with a basket full of items, I still felt I was missing something.

Whenever I feel like I need direction, I gently tune my frequency to connect with my Spirit Guides to give me a little bit of assistance. As soon as I asked the question, *What else does this person need?* the response was immediate.

Socks!

I added the thickest pair of socks I could find to my pile of items.

I left the store and made my way to the gentleman with the sign. I was nervous—not because I was afraid of the person sitting on the curb but because I was questioning if shopping for him was the right thing to do. *Maybe I should have just grabbed some cash out of the ATM and called it a day*, I thought to myself. Then I realized it wasn't nerves. It was the buzzing I had grown so used to that coursed through my body, the same buzzing that came over me before my readings as I tapped into the higher frequency needed to relay messages. It was Spirit, letting me know that I was right where I needed to be.

"Hi, what's your name?" I said to the man holding the sign.

"I'm Alec."

Alec was extremely timid, and I knew I needed to approach slowly. I tend to be very enthusiastic, especially when I'm interacting with someone new. I can only imagine what he was thinking as he saw this queer person, camp as Christmas, walking toward him with a bag full of things and an even bigger smile.

"Alec, I saw your sign, and I wanted to bring you a few things. I hope that's okay."

Alec's hand slowly reached for the bag. People driving by in their cars were staring.

"I wasn't sure what you needed, and maybe I should have asked you before I bought anything, but I hope what I got you is okay."

"Thank you," he said to me.

I nodded and walked back to my car. Through the windshield, I watched Alec go through the bag. I wondered if I'd done enough.

Should I have offered to take him somewhere? To grab him a meal? Usually, when I see a person experiencing homelessness, I'll either hand over money or buy them a snack. This moment felt a little different. I watched Alec pull out the pair of socks that I had bought for him, and he immediately took off his shoes to reveal a pair of ragged, holey old socks that had seen better days. When he peeled them off, I noticed that his toes and parts of his feet were white, as if they'd been frostbitten by the cold. He hurriedly put on the new wool socks, and as he pulled them on, a smile spread across his face.

Watching Alec excitedly put on the socks struck something within me, and I began to cry with deep sobs. Carrying out a simple act of kindness doesn't typically make me feel so emotional. Alec picked up his sign and walked away, yet I continued to sit in the car crying, wondering if I had done enough.

The next day I had a therapy appointment. The timing couldn't have been more perfect. I mean, what better time to ask your therapist why something so simple would elicit such a strong emotional response?

I recounted the experience to my therapist, Michael, everything from the text messages from the guys who weren't ready for relationships to the words I remembered my client saying to me and my encounter with Alec and the socks.

"Why was this experience so emotionally activating for me?" I asked.

"Well, why do you think it's activating?" Michael asked, repeating my question back to me as therapists have a habit of doing. Honestly, I should have predicted that he'd throw the question back at me. I do the same with my own clients and allow them to examine their own emotions in a way they might not have allowed themselves time to do otherwise. Introspection isn't the most comfortable of practices, but nudging people to look within themselves can help them in ways that simply answering their questions can never accomplish.

"I'm feeling pretty tender right now," I said honestly, "so if you could just help me out with this answer, that would be great." Retelling the story had induced more heavy crying, and I don't think I could have sorted out an explanation if I'd wanted to.

"When did you need socks and you didn't have them?" Michael asked me.

"I've always had socks," I said, confused and unsure what Michael was getting at. "Even when I was experiencing homelessness myself, I always had them."

"That's not what I mean." Michael repositioned himself in his chair and cleared his throat. I knew what I needed to hear was coming next.

"When did you need your own suffering acknowledged but it wasn't?"

"Ouch."

I knew he was right.

Like Kathy, I had been avoiding allowing myself to be helped. The previous year had been filled with so much awareness of where my own wounding was that I hadn't been taking the time to slow down and allow the Universe to show up for me. Instead, I was throwing myself into my work or filling my social calendar with men who were not emotionally available. I wasn't available to receive what I needed the most: help.

SOCKS

"I feel sad, Michael," I admitted.

"Tell me more about that sadness."

"I feel sad that there is suffering. Which is funny because I'm suffering over suffering."

Michael smiled. "And how can we soothe suffering?"

"Love."

"It's love. And so how can you allow yourself to receive love?" Michael asked.

As with most things, I knew the answer deep down. Like Kathy, I just needed the help of someone I trusted to allow me to admit it to myself. "By witnessing my own hurt and allowing myself the love that I give to others?"

"Yes," Michael said. "That's exactly it."

My session ended, and I felt peace.

That same afternoon, a package arrived at my door. It was addressed from someone I knew through Instagram. About two weeks prior, he'd reached out asking for my home address. I gave it to him without hesitation, as I'm way too trusting of strangers on the internet. He didn't tell me what he was sending, but I was about to find out.

I opened the box and found a note from him. It read: "I just thought you could use these."

In the box was a pink unicorn blanket, an ornament for my holiday tree, and a pair of thick socks. I held the socks in my hand and began to cry. I don't believe in coincidences. Spirit has taught me that this Universe is beautifully orchestrated. Two weeks earlier, none of this was on my radar. This individual felt the nudge that I needed support, and they followed the impulse. Just as I had followed my impulse that led me to Alec. Just as Kathy had followed an impulse that led her to me.

Sitting on the floor of my kitchen with the socks, the lesson became abundantly clear. I realized it wasn't about text messages or socks. It was about witnessing our own hurt and letting ourselves receive the love we need. And that sometimes the Universe will send in reinforcements if we allow it to. In this case, socks.

EIGHT

Butterflies

There's a saying about butterflies that has always stuck with me: You can spend your time chasing them, running after each one only to never quite catch them, or you can build a beautiful garden and let them come to you. *The first time I heard this, something in me clicked. In fact, it resonated so deeply that I had seven butterflies of various sizes and colors tattooed up my right rib cage as a reminder to be the garden.*

Our desires are just like those butterflies. We can exhaust ourselves chasing them down one by one, struggling, forcing situations, and never feeling truly satisfied. Or we can shift our focus to creating the right conditions in which our desires can thrive and allow the Universe to bring the right opportunities to us.

Because when we stop chasing and start *becoming* the kind of people who naturally attract what we desire, everything has a way of unfolding effortlessly. The butterflies always find the garden.

The power of our intentions is the driving force behind creating the conditions in which our desires can thrive. It's our signal to the Universe that says, "I'm here, and this is the life I came to live." An intention is powerful because it has the ability to align our thoughts, actions, and emotions and put us on a direct path to what we want to attract into our lives. When we have clear intentions, we can create lives that feel deeply connected to purpose.

What would you do differently in your life right here and now if you knew that your intention helped shape your path forward? So many people live their day-to-day lives based on subconscious programming, going with the flow and keeping their heads down. Some complain about their circumstances, and some wish that their lives could be different. I used to be one of those people. And if this is you and you are satisfied with your life, amazing! But if this is you and you wish things could be different, this could change everything for you. And I'm telling you this because it's changed my life.

I used to think that manifestation, the concept of cocreating your life through energy, was a bunch of shit. Yes, honey. I know that might sound crazy, considering it's become a part of my spiritual practice and I teach it to people. Like many folks, I read the mega-bestseller book *The Secret* in the mid-2000s, which shared that our thoughts become things and what we think is what we receive in life. My reaction? Wow, this is not going to work for me. And for a long time, I lived my life with the belief that the Universe was somehow out to get me. I also thought that the law of attraction, which is a spiritual law that says that which is like itself is drawn to it, was a bunch of marketing BS.

I can say to you with full honesty that I was wrong. It wasn't that the law of attraction didn't work. In fact, I now realize that the law of attraction was always working with me; I just didn't understand it. Like a lot of people, I thought manifestation was a means by which to acquire physical things like money, houses, soulmates, etc. (And no, this is not to say that physical things can't very much be actualizations of something greater.) But the real purpose of manifestation and intention is to live a joyful and aligned life.

This isn't a sales pitch to get you to buy into manifestation or the law of attraction. The Universe doesn't pay me a recruiting bonus for anyone who gets on board with these concepts. I'm sharing this with you because learning about the power of intention changed my life. We all have the ability to connect to this never-ending flow of energy, and it doesn't cost anything to access it. It's available to you, me, and everyone else here on this beautiful planet.

During the summer of 2020, I knew that I no longer wanted to feel the way that I was feeling, and I knew that it was time for a change. I had been leaning into unhealthy coping mechanisms that helped me to numb deeper feelings that I needed to address and heal. My desire to improve became greater than my desire to continue to numb. I wasn't living my life with any kind of meaningful intention. I was chasing the next job promotion or the next high, and it felt like a hamster wheel that I couldn't get off. My life was devoid of any real meaning. I knew that eventually I would burn out and crash. For the first time in my life, I asked myself a question that would change my entire trajectory.

What Do I Want?

Honey, I had no idea what I wanted. I only knew what I didn't want, and that would be enough to get me moving in a different direction. I knew I didn't want to continue feeling burned out, exhausted, anxious, depressed . . . I didn't want to keep feeling so empty. When we know what we don't want, it's pretty easy to identify what we do want because it's the opposite. You're broke, and you don't like it? You have a desire for more money. You're sick and don't want to be? You have a desire to be well. One day, I remembered some advice Teri, the psychic medium who'd told me that I was also a medium, had given me. She said, "Write down everything you want and focus on how it feels. Then, burn the pages." So one sunny afternoon, several weeks into my sobriety, I did just that. I grabbed a few sheets of paper and wrote down the following:

FEEL JOY

HELP PEOPLE

WRITE A BOOK

TIME FREEDOM

MONEY FREEDOM

BE PROUD OF MYSELF

That was all it took. I remember crying when I wrote those things down. For the first time in a long time, I knew what I wanted. Not what someone else wanted for me, and not something I wanted so I could make someone else proud of me. I felt a strong emotion when I thought of these things—not fear or doubt, but a deep sense of joy and gratitude. I could see myself on a stage, helping people. That feeling flooded my body with joy. I could see myself sitting at a desk, with books I had written filling the shelves behind me. Seeing and feeling all the things I was wanting to do was more than a belief that it could happen. It was a knowing that it could happen. The only thing I wasn't aware of was the how. But that didn't matter. The how is often received after you've committed to the vision.

This would be a path for me to navigate with intuition and the help of the Universe. When we declare powerful intentions, it sends a ripple of energy into the unseen world around us. Energy begins to conspire to help us, and we are met with assistance from Spirit. For me, synchronicity has been a powerful way that the Universe shows up to help. I like to think of synchronicity like the friends that Dorothy met on her journey through Oz. Each one finds her at the right time, serving a special purpose for the road ahead. Synchronicity is a powerful reminder and confirmation of our alignment with our intentions.

What I first made my list, I wasn't even remotely thinking that I would become a medium helping others connect to the light within themselves. Speaking to those who had crossed over and delivering their messages was to me not even in the realm of the possible. If you had asked me at the time what I saw myself doing, it would have been another job in the beauty industry. This is why the how or what are sometimes irrelevant because the underlying emotion of my desire lined up with something completely different from what I'd imagined for myself. And if you ask me, I'm so grateful I never got what I thought I wanted. That's the other thing about declaring an intention—we often get more than we could have hoped for. I have witnessed this time and time again, in my own life, in the lives of my clients, and also in the lives of my friends. But it's important to mention that while the energy of what we want is instantly available to us, seeing it manifest fully in our lives is a journey of unfolding.

When we set our intentions, the Universe or Spirit always provides a path. The thing is, it's not always a clear, direct path. And no one's path is the same as someone else's. One's path varies from person to person and depends on how much resistance we have in our way. Spiritual teacher Abraham-Hicks says that when we ask, it is always given, but we must be willing to let it in. When we experience things like trauma, heartache, grief, etc., we can build up resistance in our energetic, physical, and mental bodies that holds us in a place of not receiving what we truly desire. That's why healing is so important. Healing isn't so we never have to feel hurt again; it's so we can receive the life we desire. This doesn't mean you have to be fully healed to receive your desire. To paraphrase the words of one of my mentors, MaryAnn DiMarco, from her book *Medium Mentor*, healing is like the laundry—it's never done.

Zach and His Intention

One of my dearest friends, Zach, has been my greatest example of how an intention can unfold in our lives when we focus our energy on it. Zach had a strong desire to find a partner. He had zero interest in anything that was casual, and his intention was crystal clear: meet a partner who complemented his energy. As Zach's friend, I had the honor of witnessing the relationships the Universe brought him to help him prepare for his energetic match. The relationships that came to him weren't necessarily the ones that were meant to last, but all of them were meant to be.

When you declare your intention, you also tell the Universe, "I am ready to heal all that I am clinging to that is holding me back from the life I want." And the Universe will send you the opportunities to heal in the form of lessons. Sometimes, those lessons show up as people. The Universe loves sending us people to show us where our wounds are and where we can soften our edges through those relationships. Relationships are like mirrors: They reflect back the parts of us that we love, and they also reflect back the parts of us that need our love. In the case of my friend, his earlier relationships were his lessons to help him receive the kind of relationship he had been asking for.

In April 2023, my friends and I rented out a lake house to celebrate our friend Will's birthday. Anytime we all have a big sleepover to celebrate someone's birthday, I bring my tarot cards. Usually, I don't do readings for friends; though it would probably be fine to do so, I also want to ensure that I keep my own biases out of the way with people I know well. Using my tarot cards, however, helps me keep my own feelings out of the readings, and I usually joke with friends that they can blame the cards if they don't like their readings.

At the time, Zach was seeing someone who checked off almost every box on his list of what he wanted in a partner. In fact, each relationship Zach had got him closer to what was energetically ideal for him. In this case, it was nearly a perfect fit. There was just one major detail that was out of alignment. Though everything else felt right, the guy Zach was seeing wasn't emotionally available to commit to a relationship. Still, while the guy wasn't an exact fit, he was what Zach needed at the time. He was a reminder that joy and connection were still a possibility.

As I tuned in to the energy of what was needed and how I could best serve, I heard, *It's going to be in the cards; use them to channel.* Because I don't generally channel for my friends, I asked Zach for his permission, and he agreed. I laid the cards out and immediately felt a wave of knowing wash over me. "Zachy . . ." I said to him, softening my voice and preparing him for the information I was receiving. "This relationship feels like it has so many fun aspects to it. This one came along to remind you to have joy and see new possibilities." Zach had met this person after a tumultuous breakup with someone he'd felt very strongly about, and when the breakup happened, he'd had doubts about ever meeting someone he cared for as profoundly; however, a short time later, he met this new person, and their connection had so much more ease and flow. His previous relationship had taught him how to speak up for himself, and this one needed to teach him how to open his heart to miracles and possibilities after the grief of his breakup.

BUTTERFLIES

"But there's someone else coming, and that's the connection you've been manifesting." I paused and looked at my friend, unsure how he would respond. His face looked hopeful, and he smiled. He seemed almost relieved.

"Okay, great. So what do I do in the meantime?" he asked.

Just enjoy, I heard one of his Guides say.

"Enjoy it, babe. You deserve to have some fun. You've been going through this journey and have really transformed, almost like from a caterpillar to a butterfly. I believe that the next energetic match is on its way, so get ready!"

Since the person Zach was dating wasn't willing to commit to a relationship, the door was open for Zach to mingle with other folks. A few weeks later, Zach, revitalized and sure about his intention to meet his energetic match, met Ed. On their first date, Zach knew that Ed was the one he was looking for and ended the other relationship. When I met Ed, I knew this was the person Zach was meant to be with. Zach's intention had been clear. He'd not only thought his energetic match was a possibility, he could feel this connection and was ready to meet it. Just as our ears interpret vibration to sound, Zach's desire for a partner was available to be interpreted by another beautiful human.

Intention helps us align our energy with what we want to experience before we experience the physical manifestation. We are all love, interpreting love. When I started my own journey connecting to Spirit, my intention to help people felt the strongest. The love of helping people connect to the love within them, the love from their departed loved ones, and the love from Spirit became my lighthouse. That intention has been the guiding force in my life, and everything that has come from doing that—like this book, for example, or experiencing more joy—has been a wonderful by-product of that desire.

Setting our intentions and being clear about what we want to experience can also be a catalyst for deep healing. It can invite in energy that helps us release all that we are clinging to that is keeping us from the lives we genuinely want to align with. While the caterpillar doesn't know what's in store for it, it trusts in the natural cycles of life. And like that caterpillar, sometimes we must unbecome everything we have created so that we can unfold and be all that we truly are. Zach was unfolding, and the Universe was assisting his own transformation into a butterfly.

When it comes to creating the life you desire, feeling the appreciation of where you are in this moment is the big secret to living a life that feels meaningful and filled with purpose. Without that feeling, you will continue to chase the money, the relationship, the dream job—the list goes on—and no amount of these things will help you feel complete. More than happiness, joy is a state of alignment with the knowing that everything you need is within you.

Your wholeness is not defined by your manifestations. You are whole because you exist. Your miracles happen because you exist. Your energy calls them to you, and your intentions help pave the path for them to come to you. The quickest way to align with what you want is to embody the energy you want to attract. It takes more than just saying what you want. The Universe knows our hearts and our intentions. There is no faking it with the Universe. We do not receive what we talk about; we receive what we believe. Yes, what we say matters, but what we believe and know is what's doing the heavy attracting. When our words, thoughts, actions, and beliefs all align, we can create anything in our lives. If you ask me, the creating is the fun part. It's where we get to learn more about what we truly want, and we also get the honor of becoming more of who we are.

There's something so profound in the process of becoming. Your alignment with the energy of what you are asking for helps you to *be* the energetic force that attracts what you want. Embodying the energy of your intention keeps you in a state of alignment, free from feeling that you must chase down your dreams. This cocreative flow state with the Universe is the secret sauce for making dreams come true.

But what if the dream doesn't come true?

To be honest, sometimes we don't get the dreams we imagined for ourselves. "So, Travis," you might wonder, "then why have the dream at all? Won't it just end in disappointment?" But sometimes, the physical things we've asked for aren't what we need; instead, we can receive the gift of the feeling of energy that comes when we dream up our futures.

A Manifestation Come True

In late July, the boys and I took a family trip to Mexico. The special occasion was to witness Ed propose to Zach. Anytime I witness someone getting engaged or married, I can't help but think about the miracles that conspired to bring those two souls together—every decision made, every step that had to unfold, and everything in this expansive Universe that had to align perfectly.

As we walked along the beach, the warm sand beneath my feet, the scent of rain still lingering in the air, I took in the orange hues of a post-thunderstorm sunset. My friends walked ahead while I slowed down, breathing in the fresh sea air. The ocean waves moved in and out, effortless in their rhythm, and I thought about how beautiful it was that, in this moment, everything was flowing together. I knew that in just a few short moments, my friend's life was about to change forever, and I would be a witness to the power of his and Ed's aligned intentions.

One of the most beautiful honors in this life is to witness someone's journey and, in turn, have them witness yours. And here I was, watching my friend's dream come true. When Ed bent down on one knee, time seemed to slow down for just a moment. It was not lost on me that the evening had been marked by a thunderstorm followed by a breathtaking sunset—symbolizing Zach's path to his energetic match.

And as I watched Ed and Zach celebrate this life-changing moment, I finally recognized that I deserved to receive a loving relationship, too. In fact, witnessing their miracle made me realize that not only did I know that it would be possible for me, but I understood that he already existed, at least in the vibrational sense. He was out there, maybe also knowing that I was out here, too, and all I had to do now was keep tending the garden.

As I stood in that moment, fully present and filled with gratitude, a monarch butterfly gently fluttered past my head. I smiled,

BUTTERFLIES

knowing with certainty that everything was exactly as it was meant to be.

Thank you, Spirit.

NINE

September

If there's one thing I've come to understand in my work, it's this: We are never disconnected from Spirit. Not for a second. Not for a breath. Not even in the moments when we feel the most lost, the most uncertain, the most disconnected. Because connection isn't something we have to *find*—*it's something we already are. It is within each of us.*

You, as you are in this very moment, are already connected to Spirit.

You don't have to meditate on a mountaintop for hours. (I mean, you *can* if that's your thing.) You don't have to be a psychic or a medium. (Although most folks have some type of spiritual gift.) You don't have to search outside yourself for something that has been within you all along. Because Spirit isn't separate from us. Spirit isn't some external force we have to reach for, waiting for us on the other side of a curtain, dropping rewards when we're paying attention and punishing us when we're not.

Spirit is woven into *who we are.*

It's in the way love continues long after someone has left the physical world. It's in the way we instinctively *know* things without knowing *why* we know them. It's in the way our intuition nudges us toward something, the way we feel the presence of a loved one when we need them most, the way we close our eyes and sense that we are *held.*

The biggest illusion we've been taught is that we are separate—from each other, from the Universe, from the very source that created us. But that separation is a lie. We are part of something vast, something intelligent, something infinitely loving. We don't have to earn our connection to Spirit. We don't have to prove we're worthy of it. We don't have to search for a key to unlock something that has never been locked.

The connection is already within us.

And the key to feeling it? It's not about looking *outward.* It's about going *inward.*

We spend so much time looking outside ourselves for validation, for answers, for proof that we are supported. We ask for signs, we look for synchronicities, we reach for something beyond the physical world to remind us that we're not alone. And while those moments are beautiful and miraculous, they are not the sources of our connection—they are simply reflections of it. Signs and synchronicities are tools Spirit uses to remind us of their presence in our lives. They are the breadcrumbs, the gentle nudges, the cosmic winks that say, *Hey, I'm here. You're not alone.* But Spirit? Spirit isn't in the numbers on a clock or the feathers on your path. Those things are tools. Spirit is a larger energy that is the foundation of our Universe. Not only is it around you, there is a part of that energy that is also *within* you. And that piece that is within you is the cord that connects you to all that is.

That intuition that whispers truth before logic can catch up? That's Spirit.

That deep knowing that comes from out of nowhere, anchoring you in certainty? That's Spirit.

That wave of love that floods your heart when you think of someone you've lost? That's Spirit.

Spirit isn't waiting outside of you, hoping you'll notice. It's already within you, woven into the fabric of who you are, patiently waiting for you to *remember*.

So how do we strengthen this connection? How do we move beyond the illusion of separation and root ourselves in the truth that we are already whole, already held, already deeply connected to all that is?

We slow down. We listen. We trust.

We stop dismissing our inner knowing as coincidence. We stop doubting the wisdom that moves through us. We stop looking outside for answers that are already imprinted on our souls. When we get quiet—when we allow ourselves to be still, even for a moment—we feel it. That gentle hum beneath the surface, that whisper of something greater, that undeniable presence that has been with us all along.

This is why intuition feels so natural—because it is.

This is why love never dies—because it *can't*.

This is why, no matter how lost we may feel, we are never truly lost—because we are always connected.

And the remembering? It happens when we allow ourselves to trust in what we already *know*. So take a breath. Close your eyes. Feel into the space within you where Spirit already resides. That warmth? That presence? That feeling of *something more*?

That's it. That's the connection. That's you. And it has always, *always* been there.

The Unexpected Wedding Guest

"Do you remember . . . the twenty-first night of September . . ." I began singing, bobbing my head to the rhythm of the words. I love when Spirit sends me music to share with clients. I don't have a choice over what evidence I receive from the departed, but music always brings me such joy.

"Yes. That was our song," my client Michelle said with a bittersweet smile—a smile that I know all too well. It's a smile that says, "I'm grateful that my loved one mentioned this, but also, I can't believe they aren't here with me anymore." It's a smile that carries two meanings; depending on how you look at it, it can be incredibly beautiful or excruciating. But that's a part of the work that I do. I deliver messages, and while delivering them, Spirit works through me to provide comfort from grief.

Michelle was in her late twenties, and her father had made his transition into nonphysical when she was twenty-three. Her voice was light and airy, and she reminded me of a close friend of mine, someone who looked incredibly delicate, but that was just an appearance. Her energy emitted incredible strength, her outer appearance was warm, and she smiled with her entire face.

"We used to dance to it all the time when I was little. I even had it played in honor of him at my wedding. The crazy thing is that song has been playing in the most random places! In the car, the grocery store, everywhere! And it's only when I'm thinking about him."

"Well, honey, that's a synchronicity!" I shared with Michelle that our loved ones will line up signs and synchronicities for us to see as a way of saying hello or *I know you're thinking about me*. To be clear, our loved ones are not the signs or synchronicities; those are just tools. But they know we live in a material world, so they've got plenty to work with!

For just a second, Michelle seemed to drift off to another place, a place in time untouched by feelings of loss or grief, where her dad was still in a healthy physical body. Her eyes began to fill with tears, and for a quick moment, I could feel myself becoming emotional. It's important for me to not be emotional during readings—if the client and I both end up crying, it's not much of a session! For that reason, Spirit helps me hold my vibration in a state where I am not deeply connected to the information or the client—I'm just the radio receiving the signal and sharing what I receive.

Tell her I know she was with me when I passed. I was unconscious, but I knew she was there. She has always been there for me. Her father made me feel a warmth through my body, a deep sense of his love for his daughter.

"Your father is telling me that he knows you were with him when he passed." Her father showed me himself in a hospital bed with only Michelle in the room with him. She was holding his hand, crying, while he lay in the bed, nearly comatose. "He is making me feel as though he was unconscious as you sat with him in the hospital."

Travis, I had pancreatic cancer, and boy, it was aggressive. There was nothing that could be done, and my physical body deteriorated quickly. They had me on so many painkillers I didn't know up from down. The way he communicated reminded me a bit of my own dad.

Michelle's watery eyes were now full-blown crying. "I was so worried that he wasn't aware that I was there when he passed. I kept telling him that it's okay to go, and eventually, he just slipped away."

I'm with my brother. He helped me transition. She will love to hear that!

"He's also letting me know that he was welcomed into the next phase of life by his brother. Do you understand his brother being in Spirit?"

"Yes! Oh, that's so wonderful! I was hoping they would be together. They were so close growing up."

This was the first note of joy I'd heard in her voice during our session. She sat up straight and pushed her hair back.

I'm always amazed at how Spirit lets us know that not only are we deeply connected and not alone in this life but also when we depart to what's next. It's beautiful when loved ones come through to say, *Hey, I'm here with so-and-so, and please know that I'm having a great time!* In my awareness, I could feel the presence of the uncle standing with her father. I wasn't communicating with him, but I could feel him there offering love and support.

She had a beautiful wedding! She even had a picture of my handsome face out for everyone to see. I smiled as I received the energy of this soul's message.

"Honey, your dad is such a character. Did you have a picture of him out on display at your wedding?"

She nodded as she shared with me the details of her wedding day. With a smile and tears, she told me that while this was the happiest, most memorable day of her life, it was also the one day she wished more than anything that her father could have been there for. She had met someone incredibly perfect for her, and she knew that her father would have loved him. She described looking into the eyes of her future husband during the marriage vows and then, for just a moment, glancing out into the crowd of people who had come to witness their special day, hoping that just maybe she would see her father's face, that his passing had just been a dream. He wasn't there, or so she thought.

I sent the bird. This perplexed me, but then again, it's my job to deliver the mail, not necessarily to read it. Her father then showed me what looked like a crow or a raven perched on a table. I had no idea what it meant. Sometimes, it's hard to tell if Spirit is showing me a symbol or something literal, and in this case, it was literal.

"What's with the bird? It looks like a raven or a crow? Honestly, I have a hard time telling them apart. Your dad is showing it to me on top of a table."

My client had a look of absolute shock on her face. At the reception, a crow had landed on one of the guest tables, snatched some food, and flown off. Some of the guests had been terrified, while others were completely unfazed. Michelle, however, knew that the bird was more than just a bird. It was a clear sign that her dad had, in fact, come to the wedding. "And wouldn't you know, the bird swooped in while they were playing 'September.'" We both laughed hysterically, and then Michelle got quiet again.

"Travis, can I ask you something? It might be weird," she asked.

"Honey, I talk to dead people all day. Try me." I sometimes say *dead people* even though I know that they aren't anywhere near dead. It's quite the opposite. There's so much life to those in non-physical. They have returned to pure life force energy.

"I got really pissed off that my dad died. I started screaming when I was alone the other day. I couldn't help it . . . This anger came over me, and I couldn't stop myself. My neighbors could probably hear me—I was so loud. They probably think I'm some kind of lunatic, and oh my God, I can't even imagine what my dad thinks of me."

Travis, she called me an asshole, I heard her dad's voice say to me.

"Honey, who hasn't given their parent an aggressive pet name from time to time?"

She immediately burst into laughter. One of the things that Spirit does is insert humor when it's needed. It's a beautiful thing that Spirit knows when we need a laugh to lighten the energy of a session.

"I called him an asshole. What's worse is, I *think* I meant it. Well, not really in the way it sounds. I'm so mad he died. I'm so mad that he got sick and passed away, and I'm so mad that I'm mad about it. Is this normal?"

It's okay that she's angry. I love her more than words can say. She's the joy of my life, and I am so grateful that she is my daughter. I will always be with her, and she can be as angry as she needs to be. I am with her always, and "September" will be one of the many ways I say hello and let her know that I am watching over her.

I allowed every ounce of her father's loving message to flow through my body. And as the depth of the emotion and the high-vibrational frequency of the Spirit rushed through me, the energy within me began to form words, one by one, like snowflakes building into snowbanks. The energy of the words radiated to Michelle, and I could see in real time the miracle of healing happen during those moments. I watched as her shame over her anger, which had been completely natural and even appropriate, lifted from her.

Anger is a common emotion in many of my sessions when a loved one has made their transition into nonphysical. It's not necessarily anger at the person, but frustration and sorrow that they're no longer in the physical world with us. My clients are angry that loved ones can't be there for holidays, celebrations, graduations, or weddings. They are angry every time they go to text or call and then realize that their friend or partner or relative is no longer there, angry that for even a quick second they felt that their loved one was still living, only to be reminded yet again that there was no one to answer their text or call.

"Please tell him I said thank you and that I love him," Michelle said.

This is something a lot of folks do—they give me a message to pass along to their loved one. But they never really need my help. Their loved one is listening.

"You just did," I said.

She's having a baby! I heard her father say, grabbing my attention one last time.

"This is none of my business," I said, "but are you having a baby?" It was one of those moments when I really needed to lean in and trust Spirit.

"Well, we're trying, but no luck yet. Hopefully soon." Her voice was filled with hope.

"Keep me posted!" I said, feeling that Dad in Spirit may have known something that we didn't.

We concluded the session, and I thanked Spirit for the gift of healing that was given to Michelle that day. She'd begun our time together very tense and closed off; I could feel her grief coming through the computer screen—even though our reading was virtual, the energy was still palpable. By the time we concluded, she had a renewed sense of peace and love surrounding her. While I'm not able to bring a person who's passed back into a physical body, what I can do in partnership with Spirit is facilitate undeniable communication that lets someone who is grieving know that we continue beyond this physical experience and that we are always connected.

Give Me a Sign

It's easy to think of Spirit communication as just signs like pennies, feathers, repeating numbers, or in this case, a wedding-crashing bird. And don't get me wrong, signs are real. They are one of the ways our loved ones remind us they are still here, still loving us, still showing up. But our connection to those in Spirit isn't just about the big, obvious signs. It's about something much deeper. There's an invisible thread that ties us to those we love, no matter where they are.

Spirit doesn't exist in the past. They aren't stuck in some distant memory, only resurfacing when a bird swoops in to make a grand entrance. They are *now*. They are woven into our lives in ways we don't always recognize. Their presence isn't just in the undeniable moments, it's in the quiet ones, the spaces in between. It's in the way you instinctively reach for your dad's old coffee mug on a tough day. The way you hear your grandmother's voice in your head telling you exactly what you needed to hear. The way you wake up thinking about a loved one for what seems like no reason at all, only to realize it's their birthday.

The bond we share with them isn't severed by death. When someone passes on and leaves their physical body, we think the relationship ends, but it doesn't. It just changes form. We now have the honor of connecting with their truest essence, one that is free from disease, fear, and shame. We connect with the soul. The part of them that has expanded from their earthly experience and is pure, unconditional love. And their soul can share not only their love and compassion, but also what they've learned from their time on Earth.

If you think about it, love itself is invisible. You can't see it, can't hold it in your hands, can't measure it on a scale, but you *know* it exists because you feel it. It's a frequency, like music. And we are the translators of that frequency. You experience it in the warmth of a hug, in the safety of being understood, in the way someone's presence can change the entire energy of a room. That kind of love doesn't disappear. It just finds a new way to express itself through the world around us and through each other.

A roadblock people experience when trying to connect with their loved ones in Spirit is looking too hard for the signs or even dismissing them when they do appear. They want something concrete, something undeniable, like an apparition standing at the foot of their bed or a handwritten note floating down from the heavens. While I myself have witnessed many miracles, I have also dismissed my fair share of them as coincidence or happenstance. And while, sure, Spirit loves to show us in big ways that they are still with us, most of the time, the connection is subtle. It's felt, not forced.

We do not need physical signs to connect to our loved ones, though they sure give us something to marvel at. But some of my most profound experiences with Spirit happened through feelings in my body. You can feel the presence of a departed loved one in the moments when your heart swells with a memory, when a thought of them brings tears to your eyes or laughter to your lips. You feel it in the way their love shaped you, in the habits and quirks they left behind in you. If you ever doubt they're still with you, just look at yourself. You are proof of their love.

This is why grief is so heavy—it's love with nowhere to go. But here's the secret: You can still love those who have left us. You can still talk to them. You can still share your life with them. They *want* to be part of it. They are still connected to you and you to them, and that connection is infinite. So yes, the Spirit will send you signs. They'll put a bird in your path, a song on the radio, a dream that feels more like a visit than your imagination. But beyond the signs, beyond the flashes of proof, is something even more powerful: the knowing that love is eternal, that connection is never lost, and that those we love are never as far away as we think. They are right here with us, just in a different form.

And this is where synchronicity steps in. Synchronicities are the language of the Universe. They are the way the Universe weaves everything together into a masterpiece so intricate, so perfectly orchestrated, that we can't always comprehend it in the moment. But when we step back, when we zoom out, we start to see it: the connections, the patterns, the undeniable magic of how things unfold.

Some people call synchronicity a coincidence. But in my work, I've learned there's no such thing. Every time I witness those perfectly placed moments—like dominoes lining up just before the first one tips—it fills me with deep gratitude. Because it's not random, it's not accidental. It's a reminder. Synchronicity is the Universe saying, *Hey, honey, you're not alone, and you are connected to everything and everyone.*

It's Spirit whispering, *We are in this with you.*

It's the deep knowing that we are connected beyond what our human minds can fully grasp.

Think about a time in your life when things aligned in a way that felt almost too perfect. A time when you ran into the exact person you needed to meet, or when you turned on the radio and heard the words that spoke directly to your soul, when a stranger said something that answered the question you'd been silently asking the Universe. That's not luck. That's not random. That's connection in motion. That's proof that you are deeply, beautifully intertwined with something greater than yourself.

Spirit works within synchronicity to remind us of our inherent connection. They nudge, they orchestrate, they place breadcrumbs along our paths—not to control our journeys, but to remind us that we're already on the right ones. The moment we stop dismissing synchronicities as mere coincidences and start seeing them as signposts, as love notes from the Universe, is the moment we begin to *trust*—in Spirit, in ourselves, in the invisible thread that connects us all.

And the beautiful thing? This connection isn't something you have to earn. You don't have to meditate for hours or reach some enlightened state to access it. You are already connected. Always have been, always will be.

Because at the end of the day, synchronicities, Spirit, and the signs we receive aren't about proving anything. They are about *reminding* us of our connection.

Reminding us that we are loved.

Reminding us that no matter what is happening in our lives or how chaotic, uncertain, or painful it gets, there is something greater at work, aligning things in ways we can't yet see. But if you are willing to be open to possibility, and open to the belief that everything in this great big Universe is connected after all, Spirit will show you synchronicities beyond your wildest imagination.

So the next time something lines up perfectly, the next time you feel that nudge, that *knowing*, just pause. Breathe it in. Feel the moment. Say thank you. Because that's Spirit. That is the Universe showing you that you are exactly where you need to be. That's the incredible power of synchronicity. It isn't your imagination or coincidence.

And you are never, ever alone.

A Bundle of Joy

A week after Michelle's session, I received an email from her. She wanted to let me know that a few days after her session, she took a pregnancy test "just to see." Something kept nudging her that she was carrying new life, and she was right. She and her husband were delighted that she was pregnant and that her father in Spirit had known all along.

Something I'm asked often is "Do our loved ones who have departed get to meet the babies who come after their departure?" The answer is yes, they absolutely do. I've received countless confirmations from souls who have departed sharing beautiful messages for those who have had babies after their physical passing. They confirm time and again that they do meet the souls of the children who are born after they have crossed over and also care for the souls who didn't quite make it into a physical body to have an earthly experience.

Music on the Beach

The afternoon after I met with Michelle, I felt myself being nudged to recharge my energy at a local beach park in Washington.

Receiving socks was a lovely gift from the Universe, but I didn't want them to pop up as a reminder that what I really needed was more self-care. As I sat on a large piece of driftwood, watching the water flow in and out from the shore, I got to thinking about the synchronicities in my own life. For a while, my mind dismissed them as coincidence, but the more and more I dove into my own healing, the more I recognized them.

As the water rushed in and out, I noticed how perfectly synchronistically it moved to its own rhythm, the waves surging back and pushing forward. I thought about my own journey, how there were chaotic moments and times that felt completely disconnected, but actually they were pieces of a much bigger picture coming together. I thought about the way that people enter and exit our lives, how signs appear just when we are losing hope. I had spent years questioning the timing of things only to be reminded again and again that everything is right on track. I thought about the relationships that ended in heartbreak only to redirect me to something better, the random conversations with strangers that turned into lifelong friendships, or the moments I felt completely lost only to find myself exactly where I needed to be.

While I was lost in my thoughts, I had totally missed the celebration happening a few feet away from me. A family of six was listening to music and celebrating the birth of a new baby boy. I smiled at the sight of them dancing joyfully, celebrating the gift of life. It took me a moment to recognize the song they were listening to. It was "September."

SEPTEMBER

A wave crashed against my feet, and it was a perfect reminder that everything in life is always in a perfect flow, even when we can't see it. But if we are open, the Universe, or our departed loved ones, will send us signs and synchronicities, reminding us that we are never truly lost. We are just waiting for a tide to bring us back home.

TEN

My Way

Resilience is not about never failing or experiencing difficult moments in life. It's about how we choose to show up again after we do fail. Life will happen. That is not a possibility; it is a guarantee. There will be moments when everything feels like it's falling apart, when the things we thought were solid crumble beneath us, and our energy is depleted by stress and fear. The real question is not whether we will experience pain or setbacks but, rather, *How do we pick ourselves back up and show up?*

For a long time, I thought resilience meant putting on a brave face, pushing through, and not feeling discomfort during those moments of struggle. But resilience is not about pretending to be unaffected. It's not about suppressing emotions or denying pain. It's about allowing yourself to feel, to process, and then to decide that you are going to keep moving forward anyway. It's about feeling defeated or unsure about the path forward, but saying, "I have no idea what's next, but I'm showing up for myself anyway."

Resilience can feel excruciating because it requires us to have faith that everything is working out even when times are uncertain. Resilience isn't freedom from the pain of uncertainty but rather the energy we conjure up to nudge ourselves toward hope when the circumstances are less than hopeful.

I've had moments when I wanted to give up. When the unnecessary weight of judgment, loss, or uncertainty felt like too much to carry. I needed to learn how to let go of the opinions of others that didn't belong to me.

Before I had fully come out as a medium, I was given an incredible opportunity to appear on a video podcast I admired. I was ecstatic. I showed up fully as myself, poured my heart into the conversation, and left feeling proud of how I had represented my work. But when the episode aired, the comment section was brutal. People who did not even know me picked apart everything I said, mocked my work, and criticized me in ways that felt deeply personal. I told myself I shouldn't care, but the truth is it hurt deeply. During this time, my dad's dad, my papaw, was making his transition into nonphysical, and little did I know that his final words to me would help me find my own resilience.

Very Delta

My Uber pulled up to the podcast studio building near Hollywood in L.A., and I was both nervous and honored to be a part of this special episode. The host, Delta Work, is someone I admire—a drag queen who had built an impressive career for herself. She was known for her humor, her sharp wit, and most of all, her authenticity. She spoke with such clarity and never minced her words. To have a medium on her show was something new, and I was ecstatic to be invited.

This was my first time doing a podcast where the sole focus wasn't spirituality, and as I made my way into the studio and noticed images from other shows filmed here that lined the walls, I thought to myself how lucky I was to even be in the building. I could feel the energy of the building, but even more so, I had already begun to feel the energy of the departed loved ones I would be connecting with on the episode. Immediately, I felt the presence of a father figure in Spirit.

I was asked to wait in the dressing area, a space where the host also got ready before each show. Almost instantly, I felt the father's energy say to me, *I sit here while she gets ready!* I smiled, knowing that this person I admired was surrounded by the love and support of those who had passed. I kept taking long, slow breaths, keeping my energy open and trying not to let my nerves get the best of me. My own ego likes to pop up in moments like this, trying to take over. As humans, we never truly escape our egos—it's just part of the deal of being in a human body.

Over the years, I've learned to work with my ego by recognizing when it is showing up. Ego can manifest in many ways, and for me, it usually takes the form of shame or fear. Sometimes, the best thing we can do is be aware of what is happening and allow ourselves the space and grace to sit with it. As I took deep breaths,

I asked myself, *What is my ego trying to tell me? What is the truest essence of this energy?*

In order to move through difficult emotions, we have to name them. We do not have to know where they came from, but when we can identify what we are feeling, it becomes easier to soothe it or to kick it to the curb entirely. At that moment, I knew what I was feeling. It was fear.

So I asked myself another question. *What are we afraid of?*

The thing is, you cannot push against your ego. If you say, *Screw that, I'm not afraid,* your ego will just get louder. It's kind of like a screaming child. What actually helps in these moments is getting curious. *Why am I afraid?*

For me, I was afraid of messing up the reading and looking silly. I was afraid of giving incorrect information and having it captured on film. I was worried about what people would think about the reading I was about to give to Delta. I was making this moment all about me.

When we sit with our egos, we are allowing ourselves the opportunity to see things differently. There is no need to abandon the ego or fight against it. Instead, we can listen to what it has to say, acknowledge it, and from that space, we get to choose something different. And so, in that moment, I said a prayer. *God, help me see beyond this moment. Help me get out of the way so I can serve. Give me the words to serve.*

As soon as I finished the prayer, the producer came to get me from the dressing room.

It was time to serve.

The set reminded me of a late-night talk show set. Delta sat behind a desk wearing a big smile. Her energy was warm. I sat down on a beautiful cozy couch next to the desk, and we began our interview. Truthfully, I don't remember much about the interview because I was so nervous. I was in awe of her energy, and it felt wonderful to chat with her. For a moment, I forgot that cameras were recording the entire experience.

And then, it was time for the reading.

Delta had never had a reading from a medium before, and I was excited to deliver messages to her. As I began to tune in to the energy, her father stepped forward. When people watch live mediumship, whether on TV or in person, they only see the conversation happening between the medium and the person receiving the message. But there is actually a whole second conversation happening between the medium and Spirit.

Her father was showing me different parts of his body—his chest and lungs—which let me know there had been some kind of breathing issue or difficulty with the physical body. Later, we would discover this was from being exposed to Agent Orange during the Vietnam War. When I feel a delay in breath from a Spirit communicator, it is often their way of letting me know that they were not able to say goodbye before they passed.

He thanked Delta for caring for her mother and said that he had sat with Delta while she prepared for her show that day. As I shared this information with Delta, something beautiful happened. Her energy softened. I could feel her receiving what I believe was healing and comfort from her father. They'd had a difficult relationship, and Delta had been unsure if her father was proud of her. I can tell you—he absolutely was.

Sometimes, while in physical bodies, our loved ones carry their own judgments or fears. But those judgments do not follow them into Spirit. Judgments, fears, and shame are left behind with the physical body. In Spirit, only love remains.

As the reading was coming to a close, her father pointed to a wristwatch.

"Your dad is making reference to a watch," I said. "Is this something you have or that your mom has? What is it with this watch?"

Delta paused for a moment, then lifted her wrist to show me her watch—the one on her left hand, opposite from where I was sitting. It was slim, with a delicate band and a small face. She shared that in the dressing room that morning, she had wondered what she would wear if she ever had the chance to meet her dad while in drag. She decided to put on a watch, feeling for some reason that her dad would want to see her wearing one.

The room grew quiet. There was a shift in the energy—an undeniable presence of healing circulating through the space. I was so grateful to Spirit for showing up in that moment and allowing that healing to take place and for helping me get my own ego out of the way so I could deliver the message that needed to be heard that day.

Papaw

The day before the episode was set to be released, my papaw crossed over. My papaw's life had been nothing short of incredible.

He owned a pizza shop in the town where I grew up, and he was beloved throughout the community.

A month before he transitioned from his physical body, I had the gift of visiting him in the hospital. I happened to be home in Ohio when we learned that Papaw had been in the hospital for several days with COVID. My sister and I went to see him, unsure of what his condition would be when we arrived. I had a feeling—one I couldn't shake—that this would be the last time I saw him.

He was lying in his hospital bed with an oxygen mask strapped to his face to help him breathe. A nurse kept telling him to stop talking because each time he spoke, it would shift the mask and tubes, preventing him from getting the oxygen he needed. But my papaw—who had worked every day of his life, who had spent decades running Ron's Pizza in Miamisburg, who was, in every sense, a local legend—wasn't the kind of man to be told not to talk.

I had never seen him like this before. He had always been active, always moving, always telling a story. The year before, I had visited him at home while he was clearing out some of the things he and my granny had stored in the Pink Room, where we had once played with the Ouija board. He showed me the treasures he was letting go of and asked if there was anything I wanted. I selected a bell I used to ring as a child—a small reminder of Granny and her energy. That bell still sits on my desk to this day.

While my sister, who is a mom and excellent in hospital situations, asked the nurse a flurry of questions about our grandfather's condition, I just sat and looked at my papaw, knowing that soon he would be making his transition home. I could feel Granny's energy in the room with us, and I had no doubt she would be watching over him until it was his time to leave his body.

He kept trying to talk, but the oxygen monitors beeped every time his levels dropped. When it was time for my sister and me to leave, Papaw looked at me, removed his mask, and said, "I'm so proud of you. You have important work to do. Keep going. And tell your granny I said hello."

I knew those would be the last words I ever heard from him. He seemed to understand that, too.

He stayed in the hospital for a few more days, and the doctors said he was improving and would be able to go home soon. As much as I wanted that to be true, my intuition told me otherwise.

A few nights later, Granny visited me in a dream and let me know that she would be taking Papaw home. And just a few days later, his soul peacefully left his body.

When my dad called to tell me that Papaw had passed, I already knew. My heart ached for my dad. My papaw had already lost two sons—my dad's brothers, my uncles—and I knew in my heart that when he crossed over, he was greeted not only by Granny but by his sons, as well. My aunt Abbie had been with him when he took his final breaths, and she said she could feel his soul leave his body. He had tried to hold on, to stay resilient, she told us, but eventually, he surrendered to the inevitable.

Our departed loved ones teach us the most beautiful lesson about surrender. No matter how resilient we have been, eventually the time comes for us to release the temporary physical vessel we have been living in and return to our truest form: love.

I Didn't See That Coming

The day after Papaw passed was the day my *Very Delta* episode was released. What should have been a joyful moment—a career milestone—quickly became one of the most difficult learning experiences I've ever had.

There are many people who are skeptical about mediumship, and I completely understand their skepticism. But not everyone on the internet is kind. I would have settled for skepticism, but some of the comments on this video were worse. Unfortunately, social media can be a volatile place. It can also be a beautiful one—it just depends on how you choose to use it.

One of my friends messaged me after watching the episode. He wrote, "Gosh, Travis, that was such a great episode. But yikes, the comments."

I knew better than to read the comments on a YouTube video.

But I did it anyway.

So there I was—grieving the loss of my grandfather *and* reading the unkind words of strangers on the internet. And these weren't just skeptical comments. They were *vicious*.

I had felt so good about the reading. It was my first time delivering messages in this kind of format, and I was so excited and proud of the work I had done. But some viewers had very different opinions.

Some called me a grifter. A scam artist. Some attacked my appearance. The sound of my voice.

And the part that stung the most? These were members of *my own* LGBTQ+ community. The very people I hoped would support me were the ones tearing me apart. I read the comments one by one, letting each cruel remark sink in. And even though there were plenty of lovely, supportive comments, my focus went straight to the mean and cutting ones. Reading the remarks sent me into a two-day spiral. I barely left my bed. I was crying over the loss of my grandfather, crying over how *mean* people could be. My mind raced, replaying the comments over and over again on a loop. *Grifter. Scam artist. Annoying voice.* Over and over.

And I started to wonder—did I want to keep doing this? Did I want to keep subjecting myself to this kind of criticism? Could I handle knowing that no matter how much love I put into my work, there would always be people ready to tear me down?

As I lay in bed having my own pity party, the book *Daring Greatly* by Brené Brown popped into my mind. I hadn't read it in some time, but something told me to grab it off the shelf—there was something in that book I needed to read.

In *Daring Greatly*, Brené talks about the power of owning our stories, what happens when we face our shame and fear head-on, and how we must keep showing up anyway. Even though we might be feeling down and out, we always have the choice to rise again. There will always be folks who criticize from the bleachers but are too afraid to get in the arena themselves.

I was in the arena.

And then I thought of my papaw.

He was in business for himself for fifty years, running a pizza shop in a small town in Ohio. He showed up to work *every single day*. No matter what was happening, no matter what was going on in his life, he was there—making sure the business was running, doing what he loved. And in that moment, I realized—that's exactly what I needed to do.

Yes, this moment was difficult. And yes, there were going to be more difficult moments. Because anytime you show up in the world as yourself—sharing your gifts, putting your heart into something—you open yourself up to people's opinions and criticisms. But I don't believe for one second that that should be enough of a reason to give up on something you love.

And I *knew* I loved helping people.

I *knew* I loved mediumship.

The Words That Changed Me

Later that week, I had my therapist check in with Michael. I poured my heart out—about the comments from the *Very Delta* episode, how they made me feel, and the grief I was still processing from losing Papaw. I've always believed that my Guides sometimes reach me through my therapist, and that day was no exception.

He looked at me and said words that, in that moment, changed everything.

You see, my deepest fear wasn't just that people were being cruel. It was something deeper, something I hadn't fully acknowledged before. It was the fear that their opinions somehow had the power to strip me of my gift. That their viciousness could take away something I hold so dearly: the gift of helping people.

Michael took a deep breath, looked me straight in the eyes, and said, "Travis, when you have a gift from the Universe, no one can take that from you. And your job is to show up. No matter what people say. No matter if you're in a room of two or two thousand. That gift is in you for a reason."

And there it was—the exact reminder I needed.

The comments, the opinions, the noise—they didn't actually have power over me. Not unless I gave it to them. At the core of my fear wasn't a question of whether I was good enough, because this work isn't about me. And the reality is I'm not for everyone—and that's okay. I don't need to convince anyone. I don't need to prove anything. The people who are meant to find me will. The people who are meant to receive healing will. And those who don't believe? They were never part of the equation to begin with.

As long as I feel aligned with the work I'm doing and stay committed to showing up, and as long as I keep my heart open and my intentions clear, no one can take this gift from me.

And that realization? That was freedom.

And even though some people didn't like the reading I gave to Delta, *I* thought it was good. More important, Delta received the healing she needed, and that was what mattered most. It wasn't about what strangers on the internet had to say. It was about *whether the person receiving the reading got what they needed.* That was the only thing that truly mattered.

And then, I heard my grandfather's words replay in my ears: *I'm so proud of you. You've got important work to do.*

I got out of bed. I took a shower. And I decided that day that my resilience didn't have to mean carrying the pain and weight of other people's opinions. I could surrender to the knowing that people were *always* going to have opinions about the work I do. And I was going to have to find a way to move forward despite them.

And then I wondered—would my papaw have given up his business and walked away from what he loved, just because someone had given him a negative review?

What I know for sure is that he *wouldn't*.

And he certainly didn't.

A Life Well Lived

Two weeks later, I went home for Papaw's funeral. As we followed the hearse from the funeral home to the cemetery, people lined the streets for blocks to say their final goodbyes to my grandfather's physical vessel. When we drove past his restaurant, there were even more people—holding signs, placing flowers, paying their respects to the man who had shown up *every single day* for his community.

I sat in the car with my dad, both of us in awe at the sheer number of people who had come to honor him. All their lives had been touched by my papaw. People showed up for him, just as he had shown up for them.

During the funeral, someone spoke about my papaw's vision for the town we grew up in. I remember the words distinctly: "Ron saw Miamisburg not for what it was but for what it could be."

And in that moment, I *knew*. That was his secret—not just to his resilience but to his *success*. He saw the bigger vision. He *held* that vision in his heart. And he *showed up* every single day, no matter the circumstances, driven by his mission to serve.

At the end of the service, they played "My Way" by Frank Sinatra. As the words *I did it my way* played softly—against the backdrop of quiet sobs and gentle rain falling—I thought to myself, *Yes, you did, Papaw.*

And I would, too.

Taking My Power Back

The people who criticize from the sidelines are afraid. Those who tear others down are often the same ones who are too scared to put themselves out there, to chase the lives they truly want. It's easier to judge than to risk. It's safer to project fear onto others than to face it within us.

If I had stayed in bed and let their words define me, I would have been handing my future over to *their* fear. I would have been letting *their* doubts dictate *my* path. But that's not how resilience works.

We take our power back when we show up *anyway*—when we stand tall despite the setbacks, when we refuse to let someone else's fear shrink our light. Because at the end of the day, the loudest voices of doubt are never from the ones doing the work. They come from the ones watching, wishing they had the courage to do it, too.

Our setbacks can serve us—if we let them. They can be springboards for massive growth, but it all comes down to how we choose to view them. A setback can keep you in bed for days, drowning in self-doubt, or it can be the catalyst that realigns you with your vision. It can distract you from your desire, or it can fuel your next step forward.

The truth is we always have a choice, even in the moments when it feels like we don't. We can let our setbacks define us, or we can let them refine us. One way keeps us stuck. The other moves us closer to the lives we're meant to live.

Resilience is choosing to stand back up, even when it feels impossible. It is deciding that your purpose is greater than your fear. It is understanding that failure, rejection, and setbacks are not signs to stop but rather signs that you are *in the game*. We all have moments when we fall, and sometimes, we stay down longer than we would like because that downtime might be much-needed rest. But eventually, we get to make the choice to get back up. Not because it's easy, not because we have everything figured out, but because there is still more ahead of us.

Resilience isn't just about overcoming difficult moments—it's about *choosing* to keep going, even when doubt, criticism, and uncertainty threaten to pull you under. And in my journey as a medium, resilience has been the invisible thread woven through every challenge, every breakthrough, and every moment I've had to pick myself up and remind myself: *This work matters. Keep going.*

Being a medium requires a level of resilience that many people don't fully understand. It's not just about connecting with Spirit—it's about holding space for grief, offering validation in a world that often demands proof for things that can only be *felt*, and trusting what I receive even when others question it. That's not always easy. It takes courage. It takes trust. And it takes the willingness to keep showing up, even when others don't understand or accept what I do. But truthfully, I'm not sure of any profession that doesn't receive criticism.

My belief in the power of healing is bigger than my fear. My trust in the work, in Spirit, in the transformation that happens when we open ourselves to something greater—it outweighs the doubt, the criticism, the fear of being seen. And that is what keeps me showing up.

There have been moments when my confidence was shaken—when skepticism, both from others and from within, made me question my path. I've faced criticism from strangers on the internet and from people who have dismissed my work without ever experiencing it. There have been times when the weight of other people's fears and projections made me wonder if it was all worth it. And yet, I continued because I believe in something greater than myself.

That's resilience.

It's in the moment I chose to get out of bed after deciding not to let strangers define my worth. It's in the moments I stood on a stage with shaking hands and trusted Spirit to work through me. It's in the way I continue to evolve, refining my gifts, deepening my connection, and showing up—not because it's easy, but because it's *mine*.

Resilience is in surrendering—to the unfolding of my path, to the lessons Spirit teaches me, to the moments when I have to let go of control and trust that I am *exactly* where I need to be. It's in knowing that even when I feel exhausted, even when my faith wavers, even when the work feels heavy—I am still *called* to do the work.

It's in remembering that my work is bigger than the noise.

Connection is why I keep showing up.

It's why I keep trusting the bigger vision.

It's why I'm still here, still delivering messages and bringing healing.

And just like my papaw, who showed up for his community every single day with a vision bigger than himself, I show up for the people who need me. Because that's what resilience is.

But resilience isn't just about showing up for *others*—it's about showing up for *myself*, too. It's about recognizing when I'm letting fear take the driver's seat and choosing to take my power back. Fear creeps in, trying to keep us safe, but too often, we let it become the loudest voice in the room.

It doesn't have to be.

Resilience isn't about ignoring fear or pretending it doesn't exist. It's about *honoring* it, *acknowledging* it, and choosing to move forward anyway. Because growth doesn't come from staying comfortable—it comes from stepping into the discomfort, trusting that something greater is waiting on the other side. That's not only resilient, it's an act of love.

And that's what I am. And you are, too.

Resilience isn't about avoiding the fall or the lesson. Setbacks can be the greatest assets to your growth if you allow them to be. Your setbacks can serve you and set you free—as long as you trust yourself enough to *show up*—again, and again, and again. Resilience is knowing that no matter what happens, your worth remains unchanged.

Because you are worthy simply because you *exist*.

And nothing—no setback, no mean comment on the internet, no fear—can take that away.

Keep showing up and keep doing it your way.

ELEVEN

Heaven Is a Place on Earth

Before I step on stage for a live mediumship demonstration, my walk-out music is "Heaven Is a Place on Earth" by Belinda Carlisle. Why? I'm so glad you asked. It's a reminder that heaven isn't some distant place; it's here in the love, connection, and healing we experience. And also, the song raises my vibration every time I hear it.

Abundance is our birthright. It's not something we have to earn or hustle for. It's something that is always available to us. Most of the time, when people hear the word *abundance*, they think of money. I used to associate abundance with money, too. And sure, financial abundance is wonderful and helpful—especially considering we live in a material world. But that's not the kind of abundance I'm referring to.

I'm talking about abundance in all forms—the abundance of air, of connection, of those warm, fuzzy feelings that rush through you when something brings you joy. Abundance is an energy we have the ability to tap into whenever we choose. And like anything else, when we get the energy of abundance rolling in one area of our lives, it starts spilling over into all the other areas, too.

When I was growing up, I was taught that heaven was a physical place—a place with mansions, fluffy clouds, and everything we could ever desire at our fingertips. My first introduction to this concept came when our family dog Heidi needed to be put to sleep. She was a gorgeous German shepherd who would let me snuggle up against her in the mornings before my parents were awake.

When she crossed over, my mom comforted me with a beautiful story about where Heidi was going so that she could rest—where one day, we'd be able to visit her. It was a place where there was only joy and love and we could have anything we ever wanted. Heaven sounded like an incredible place, but one question lingered in my mind: Why did we have to wait until we died to experience its incredible abundance?

The truth is—we don't.

What I have been shown of the other side is that heaven isn't necessarily a physical place—it's a frequency. It's a vibration in which our energy exists. It's a space we move through beyond the limitations of physical bodies, beyond time as we know it.

And while I believe we have access to this incredible energy right here, right now, I don't believe it makes us immune to suffering on Earth. Our souls—the essence of our energy—came here to experience something we couldn't experience from the heaven frequency. That thing? Contrast.

Contrast is what fuels our growth. It's the lessons, the challenges, the things that shake us up and make us expand. It's what pushes us forward. But contrast can also push us into suffering if we allow it to.

I remember a session with a client who had told a friend that she felt that her lot in life was to suffer—that maybe she wouldn't feel relief until she left her physical body. Her Spirit Guide came through and said, *Why are you waiting to cross over to feel joy?*

We don't have to wait.

We have a divine right to feel joy right now. We have a divine right to experience abundance in this lifetime.

We don't have to wait until we separate from these bodies to feel the freedom, love, and light that our souls already know. Heaven isn't somewhere we go—it's a frequency we align with.

Earlier, I described the day I gave up drinking—the day I found myself lying on my floor after a three-day vodka bender. I asked God, the Universe, *What do I do?* And in the stillness, through the haze and the weight of it all, I heard one word: *Meditate.*

So I sat with myself in the quiet, in the wake of everything I had been numbing. But also, in that meditation, I did something I hadn't done in a long time—I prayed. I didn't pray for the pain to go away or for things to magically fix themselves. Instead, I asked the Universe to use me. To allow me to serve others, to help people in a way that mattered. And in return, I asked to feel full. Because I was so tired of feeling empty. I didn't have the language for it at the time, but looking back, I now recognize that as my moment of surrender.

I wasn't just giving up alcohol—I was surrendering my emptiness. I was trading it in for purpose. For service. For a life that actually felt abundant. Today, I can tell you with full honesty—I still feel that emptiness sometimes. The difference is now I know what to do with it. I know how to tune myself to something that feels more abundant. Not by forcing myself to be happy or pretending the emptiness isn't there, but by recognizing it, sitting with it, and choosing—when I'm ready—to shift.

It's not about never feeling lonely. And there will always be times when we experience grief or emptiness. It's about having the tools to tune in to a frequency of relief.

Is it always this simple? No. And I would be sorely misleading you if I didn't acknowledge that trauma, depression, anxiety, and grief can make even the smallest sliver of joy feel impossibly far away. Sometimes, just reaching for neutrality—something *slightly* lighter than the weight we're carrying—is all we can do. And that's okay. That neutrality can still open the door for massive amounts of abundance. The Universe doesn't expect you to be jumping for joy 24-7.

But what I want you to know—what I need you to know—is that joy and abundance are always possible. No matter where you are on your journey. No matter how far away they may seem. They are not just reserved for people who have it all together. They are yours, too.

You don't have to reach for joy all at once. Just reach for the next best feeling. One small shift at a time. That's where abundance begins.

Abundance: The Art of Receiving

I used to think abundance was something you *achieved*. If you worked hard enough, manifested hard enough, or just *got your life together*, money, opportunities, and all the good things would come flooding in. But here's what Spirit has taught me—abundance isn't a finish line. It's not something you arrive at or unlock like a video game level. It's an *energy*. A frequency. A way of being that exists whether your bank account is overflowing or you're eating ramen and hoping your car makes it another week without a new mystery noise.

And trust me, I've been on both sides of that equation—especially the latter part of that equation. A good part of my late teens/early twenties was spent with my Check Engine light on and scraping together enough change from the floorboards of my car to buy a burger from McDonald's.

There was a time in my life when I was constantly chasing abundance, convinced that if I could just hustle hard enough, say the right affirmations, and prove to the Universe that I was worthy, then I'd finally be taken care of. I would finally *be* worthy. And there would be times when I earned decent sums of money, but it went out as quickly as it came to me. I'd look at other people who seemed to have it all—money, love, opportunities—and wonder, *What do they know that I don't?* I felt I was on the outside looking in, always a few steps behind where I wanted to be.

But abundance doesn't respond to desperation. It responds to *trust*. To alignment. To the energy of *already having* instead of always needing more. Abundance is a knowing that what we have is enough. And if we are always looking elsewhere for abundance, or thinking we know what it looks like, we won't see it when it's right in front of our noses.

One of my favorite parables captures this very conundrum, the way that our team in Spirit sends us what we are asking for, just not what we are expecting.

> *A storm descends on a small town, and the downpour soon becomes a flood. As the waters rise, the local preacher kneels in prayer on the church porch, surrounded by water. By and by, one of the townsfolk comes up the street in a canoe.*
>
> *"Better get in, Preacher. The waters are rising fast."*
>
> *"No," says the preacher. "I have faith in the Lord. He will save me."*
>
> *Still the waters rise. Now the preacher is up on the balcony, wringing his hands in supplication, when another guy zips up in a motorboat.*
>
> *"Come on, Preacher. We need to get you out of here. The levee's gonna break any minute."*
>
> *Once again, the preacher is unmoved. "I shall remain. The Lord will see me through."*
>
> *After a while the levee breaks, and the flood rushes over the church until only the steeple remains above water.*

The preacher is up there, clinging to the cross, when a helicopter descends out of the clouds, and a state trooper calls down to him through a megaphone.

"Grab the ladder, Preacher. This is your last chance."

Once again, the preacher insists the Lord will deliver him.

And, predictably, he drowns.

A pious man, the preacher goes to heaven. After a while he gets an interview with God, and he asks the Almighty, "Lord, I had unwavering faith in you. Why didn't you deliver me from that flood?"

God shakes his head. "What did you want from me? I sent you two boats and a helicopter."

The Illusion of Not Enough

One of the biggest lies we tell ourselves is *I don't have enough*. Not enough money, not enough time, not enough love, not enough talent. That belief alone is one of the biggest blocks to abundance because it keeps us in a constant state of lack—always waiting for something external to complete us.

I remember a time when I was hustling for readings, feeling I had to say yes to every opportunity because if I didn't, the bookings would dry up. I was overworking, undercharging, and completely ignoring the fact that I was drained. In my mind, I couldn't afford to slow down. Because what if I did and the clients stopped coming? What if the money disappeared?

Spoiler alert: That fear-based energy wasn't helping me attract more abundance. It was doing the opposite.

Abundance doesn't come from scrambling. It comes from *trusting that you're already supported*. And I know—trusting when you feel broke or stuck is the hardest damn thing to do. But it's also what shifts everything.

How Spirit Taught Me That Abundance Is an Energy

One of the biggest turning points for me came through a client reading. Spirit has this way of calling me in even when I'm the one doing the reading, and on this particular day, I got a lesson I wasn't expecting.

I was reading for a woman who had spent her whole life struggling financially. She'd grown up in survival mode, always worried about making ends meet, and that energy had followed her into adulthood. As I connected with her father in Spirit, he came through with a booming presence. He wasn't subtle—he was direct, loud, and completely unfiltered (which I personally love in Spirit). He also just happened to be an entrepreneur who had left his daughter several businesses that had been financially successful until his departure. The businesses started to decline once his daughter, my client, took them over, and of course she believed that she was responsible for the loss.

He said, *She has to stop waiting to feel rich. She has to feel rich first.*
I paused. *Wait . . . What?*

He went on: *Abundance isn't about what's in your wallet. It's about what's in your energy. If she keeps acting like she's broke, she'll stay broke, and so will the businesses. But if she walks through the world knowing she's taken care of, everything will change.*

And that hit me hard because I realized—he wasn't just talking to her. He was also talking to *me*.

I shared with her what her father had said and described him as I saw him: dressed in a nice suit and holding his head high.

She said, "Dad would always put on a suit when funds started to dry out. He said it was his 'mojo money suit.'"

And there it was.

I had been carrying around the same energy of *waiting* for abundance. Waiting for proof that I was supported. Waiting for the external validation before I believed I had enough. But you don't get proof first. You shift your energy first, and then the Universe meets you there.

Shifting into Receiving Mode

But what does that actually mean? How do you go from feeling broke and stuck to feeling *abundant* when your reality doesn't reflect it yet? In the book *Ask and It Is Given*, spiritual teacher Abraham-Hicks shares that the Universe always delivers the vibration of the physical manifestation immediately. It's up to us to then receive or allow that physical manifestation to happen.

It starts with the energy of *receiving*.

And this doesn't only apply to receiving material things or improving our lives. It also applies to feeling the connection to our departed loved ones and our Spirit Guides. I believe our connections to those in Spirit help us to keep our energy open to receiving.

Most people think they have an abundance problem, but what they actually have is a receiving problem. We're so used to believing we have to earn everything—that we have to prove we deserve it, struggle for it, or wait until some cosmic scoreboard says we're worthy. But the Universe isn't withholding abundance from you—it's constantly trying to give it to you. The question is: *Are you actually open to receiving it?* And this isn't always something that's easy to be honest with ourselves about.

For me, receiving meant learning to pause and let things come to me instead of constantly forcing an issue. It meant changing my self-talk from *I need more* to *I already have so much*—even when my external circumstances weren't ideal. It meant saying yes because I genuinely wanted the opportunity instead of agreeing from a place of scarcity. It meant being aware of when I was asking for opportunities but turning them down or running from them when I didn't feel worthy of receiving them. And most of all, it meant letting abundance be easy instead of something I had to suffer for.

The moment I stopped scrambling, everything shifted. Clients started booking effortlessly. Opportunities started presenting themselves in ways I never could have planned. Money started flowing in, and instead of tapping my foot wondering when loving relationships, whether friendships or something romantic, would find me, I *trusted* that they were always on the way. And guess what? They were. And still are. But more important than seeing the physical manifestations show up in my reality, *I felt good.*

Abundance Is a State of Mind, Not a Destination

If you take nothing else from this chapter, take this: *Abundance is not something you chase. It's something you allow.*

It's not about having millions in the bank (though, let's be real, that's nice, too). It's about feeling *full*—full of possibility, full of gratitude, full of knowing that everything you need is already within reach. It's about recognizing that you're already rich in ways that money can't buy. And that you are connected to an endless stream of energy.

You are rich in connection.

You are rich in talent.

You are rich in opportunities waiting to unfold.

And the more you embody that energy, the more abundance *has no choice* but to flow to you. So as you move through this chapter, I want you to do something radical. I want you to stop waiting for permission to feel abundant. *Claim it now.* Feel it now. Live as if everything you desire is already on its way—because it is.

And if you need proof, just ask Spirit. They'll remind you.

Spirit Guides and Shifting Limiting Beliefs: Transformation at Its Best

Your Spirit Guides are *obsessed* with your success. I need you to understand this. They are not neutral. They are not waiting for you to suffer enough before they help. They're not sitting in the clouds with their arms crossed, saying, *Well, when Travis finally figures it out, maybe we'll send him a sign.* No, honey. They are constantly working behind the scenes, rearranging the chessboard, dropping breadcrumbs, and practically waving neon signs in front of your face.

The problem? Most of the time, we don't see it.

Not because Spirit isn't communicating, but because we're too busy arguing for our limitations. We all have *stories* about who we are and what's possible for us. And most of the time, those stories are loaded with limiting beliefs we picked up from childhood, society, or experiences that made us doubt ourselves. Somewhere along the way, we absorbed the idea that life is supposed to be hard, that abundance is for *other* people, and that we have to earn or prove our worth before we get to experience success, love, joy, and ease.

And our guides? They're like, *Sweetie . . . that's not how this works.* And through your connection, you can transform.

The Lies We Tell Ourselves About Abundance

A monumental shift I had to make in my own life was realizing that abundance wasn't something I had to chase after or create, it was something I needed to align with. But alignment means breaking up with the beliefs that keep you small, and let's be real, most of us are way too comfortable with our excuses.

I've heard (and said) it all:

I'll never make enough money doing what I love.
I'm just not lucky like other people.
Success takes struggle and suffering.
I can't charge that much for my services—it feels selfish.
People like me don't get opportunities like that.

Sound familiar? It should. Because almost everyone has some version of these thoughts running in the background, whether they realize it or not. Now, let me be clear: These beliefs aren't *your fault*. We don't play the blame/shame game in this house. They were likely handed down to you by well-meaning parents, teachers, or society. But here's the thing—just because a belief *feels* true doesn't mean it *is* true.

And that's where Spirit Guides come in.

How Spirit Guides Help Shift Limiting Beliefs

Your Guides' job isn't to fix you (because, news flash, you're not broken). Their job is to hold up a mirror and remind you of what's possible. They will send signs, synchronicities, and nudges in the right direction, but they can't override your free will. If you're determined to believe you're not good enough, they can't force you to see otherwise. They can only keep showing you clues until you finally start paying attention.

For example, let's say you've been struggling with money and feeling that you'll never have financial security. Your guides might:

Send you repeated angel numbers (like 888, which represents financial abundance).

Put you in situations where you hear conversations about shifting your money mindset.

Drop opportunities in your lap—but if you're still stuck in a this-is-too-good-to-be-true mentality, you'll dismiss them.

Nudge you toward a book, a podcast, or a random social media post that perfectly addresses your current struggle.

The question is: *Are you paying attention?* Or are you immediately dismissing the signs and going back to the same old story?

Noticing Your Automatic Thoughts

Our limiting beliefs aren't just *thoughts*—they're deeply wired neural pathways, and they run on autopilot until we consciously interrupt them. Dr. Tara Swart's work in her book *The Source* aligns beautifully with spiritual teachings on abundance and manifestation. It's not that the Universe is withholding abundance from us, she tells us—it's that our brains have been conditioned to *expect* struggle, lack, or limitations. And the more we repeat those thoughts, the stronger those neural pathways become.

But the best part? *Neuroplasticity means we can rewire our brains.* We can literally train our minds to default to possibility instead of fear. To expect abundance instead of lack. To shift from *Why does this always happen to me?* to *How is this working in my favor?*

This is where *awareness* becomes our superpower. If we can catch those automatic scarcity thoughts in the moment—before they spiral—we can start to replace them with something more expansive. At first, new, expansive thoughts around abundance, like *Abundance is my birthright* or *The Universe always provides me with what I need* might feel fake or uncomfortable. But with repetition, those new thoughts become just as automatic as the old ones. And that's when everything changes. Because suddenly we're not *forcing* abundance. We're simply aligning with it. The same goes for our connection to those who have departed.

For example:

If someone tells you about an amazing opportunity, do you immediately think, *That would never happen for me?*

If you see someone thriving in your field, do you feel inspired, or do you think, *There's no room for me?*

When you receive unexpected money, do you trust it, or do you immediately think, *This won't last?*

Your knee-jerk reactions will tell you everything you need to know about your current belief system. And your Guides? They're not here to judge you for those thoughts. They're just gently reminding you that you don't have to keep believing them.

The Power of Choosing a Different Story

One of the greatest lessons I've learned from Spirit is that *beliefs are just thoughts we keep thinking.* That's it. They're not universal truths. They're just repeated patterns. And if a belief is just a thought on a loop, that means you can change it.

But here's the kicker—you don't have to make some massive leap from *I'm broke* to *I'm a billionaire* overnight. Your brain won't buy it, and your energy won't align with it. The key is to find the *next best thought* you can believe.

In other words, if *I'll never have enough money* is your current belief, you don't have to force yourself to believe *I'm wildly wealthy* right away. But you *can* gently move toward:

Money has come to me in unexpected ways before—it could happen again.

There are people in my industry making great money, so it's clearly possible.

I'm open to receiving more, even if I don't know how it will happen yet.

See the difference? It's not about forcing positivity. It's about opening the door for possibility.

Letting Spirit Work Through You

One of the biggest shifts I've made in my life is learning to let my Guides work *through* me instead of *against* me. And by that, I mean trusting that when I release my grip on control, things actually flow better than when I try to force them. There it is... Surrender. And that also means learning to listen to the guidance that's already showing up for you.

So if you've been feeling stuck, here's what I want you to do:

1. **Pay attention to your automatic thoughts.** What limiting beliefs are running in the background?

2. **Notice where Spirit is already guiding you.** Are you seeing repeated signs? Hearing the same message from multiple sources?

3. **Choose a slightly better thought.** You don't have to believe in miracles overnight—just pick a belief that feels *a little* more expansive than where you are now.

4. **Practice the energy of receiving.** Stop blocking yourself with *how* things should unfold and instead ask, *What if it could be easy? Or easier than it is right now?*

You Are Always Supported

Your Spirit team is always rooting for you. They want you to win. They want you to step into your purpose, your joy, your abundance. And the only thing standing between you and the life you want? The belief that you can't have it.

But you can.

So stop arguing for your limitations and start opening up to possibility. Spirit is waiting. And they've got a whole damn cheering section just for you.

The Human Experience and Free Will

One day, I got *pissed* at the Universe.

I turned on the news and saw a city being bombed—children suffering because of decisions they had nothing to do with. In the same broadcast, a school shooting was being reported. My heart broke, my stomach clenched, and something inside me snapped.

How could this happen?

How could God/Spirit/the Universe allow this?

I wasn't just sad—I was *furious*. My ego was activated, my sense of justice was screaming, and I demanded an answer. I wanted to know, right then and there, how a Universe that I believed to be abundant, loving, and whole could allow so much suffering. I wanted Spirit to explain itself.

But I didn't receive my answer that day.

I couldn't. My energy was nowhere near the space of being able to receive it. I was too in it—too raw, too emotional, too consumed by my own outrage. And so the answer didn't come. Not that day, not that week.

I had to sit in that energy of frustration for a while. I had to wrestle with it, let it move through me, let myself feel all the things—anger, helplessness, grief—before I could even get a glimpse of relief around this topic. It wasn't an easy process, and it wasn't quick. But eventually, the answer found me.

First, let's talk about one of the biggest spiritual truths: *We live in a free-will Universe.* That means that while we are all born with divine potential and access to abundance, we also live in a world where people's choices, actions, and collective energies shape reality. We might be the center of our own universes, however we are not the center of *the* Universe.

Some souls come into this life to experience deep contrast. Some are here to break generational cycles of poverty, some to challenge the systems that create inequality, and others to be examples of resilience, love, and transformation despite the hardships they face.

Does that mean Spirit *wants* suffering? Absolutely not. But Spirit also doesn't interfere with free will, and unfortunately, human-made systems—government, economy, power structures—aren't always aligned with divine abundance.

The Collective Energy of Scarcity and Fear

One of the biggest barriers to global abundance is that *human consciousness is still deeply rooted in scarcity and fear*. We've been taught, for generations, that resources are limited, that some people are "more deserving" than others, and that wealth and success come at the expense of someone else.

This kind of thinking keeps entire systems in place that perpetuate inequality—keeping people in cycles of poverty, keeping resources concentrated in the hands of a few, and making people believe they are powerless to change their circumstances.

But here's what Spirit has shown me: *Scarcity isn't the natural order of things*. It's a *human-made illusion*. If we all believed, deep down, that there is more than enough to go around, that abundance is a collective experience rather than an individual one, and that no one is more deserving than another, we would dismantle the structures that create suffering.

Karma, Soul Contracts, and the Bigger Picture

I also believe that some souls choose difficult experiences in this lifetime for their own soul growth. That doesn't mean suffering is *deserved*—it means that, from a soul perspective, every experience (even the painful ones) is an opportunity for growth, transformation, and awakening. Our souls are not here for the comfort of our own egos.

Does that mean we just accept suffering and say, "Oh well, it's their karma"? Hell no. It means that those of us who *are* aware of abundance have a responsibility to help shift the energy—not just for ourselves, but for others.

Some people will live their entire lives in struggle, not because abundance isn't available to them, but because their circumstances, beliefs, or societal conditions make it nearly impossible for them to feel they have access to it. And that's where collective healing comes in.

What Can We Do?

Challenge the scarcity mindset in our own lives. Every time we choose abundance, generosity, and expansion over fear, we shift the collective energy.

Give back where we can. Abundance isn't just for us—it's meant to be shared. Whether that's through donations, volunteering, or just using our platforms to spread awareness, we can be part of the shift.

Hold the vision for a better world. A world where resources are more evenly distributed, where success isn't about who you were born to but how you show up in the world, where no one has to prove their worth to receive what they need.

The world isn't broken. Humanity is awakening to the truth that abundance is meant for all, not just a few. We're getting there. One shift at a time.

Bring Me a Higher Love

My answer to my big question about horrible things happening in the world came unexpectedly in a meditation one Sunday evening.

Most Sundays, my friends and I have a tradition—we gather for dinner, catch up on life, and just be together. I met each of them before I got sober and before I fully stepped into my gifts—before I really understood what healing even meant. Over time, they've become more than just friends; they're my family.

On that night, as I looked around the table, listening to their stories, their laughter, the details of their weeks, a thought hit me: Heaven was right here—a moment—a laugh shared between friends. Maybe the afterlife wasn't *after* at all. Maybe it was woven into the now, into the love we give, the trust we surrender to, and the way we show up for each other—one message at a time.

And in that moment, I felt it as a knowing: *I am abundant*. Not because I worked for it, not because I had to prove myself, but simply because I *am*. I finally let myself fully receive.

That's the funny thing about surrendering to the Universe—it always seems to know exactly what we need, even when what we receive looks nothing like what we had in mind for ourselves. I was far from where I had begun my journey, but I had never felt more like home. Maybe I didn't know why things happened in the world the way they did, but maybe I didn't need to know. All I needed to know was that I was going to show up with love, and that would be what guided me.

After dinner, once everyone had left and the house was quiet, I sat down to meditate. I let myself sink into gratitude—for the privilege of serving Spirit and helping people reconnect with their loved ones, for the friends and chosen family who see me fully, and for the simple but profound gift of being *me*. No hiding, no filtering—just me.

And then, the answer I had been looking for came.

It came from my Guides, but only after I finally released my grip on demanding to know why Spirit lets these things happen in the world. Only after I stopped trying to wrestle the Universe into an explanation that would make sense to my human mind. And when the answer arrived, it was simple.

Sometimes, God uses you all as the rowboat.

And just like that, I remembered the rowboat story.

I remembered that Spirit or God is not separate from us. It's not some external force watching from a distance, deciding when to step in and when to stay silent. Spirit is within us. In our hands. In our words. In the way we show up for one another. And if that's the belief we hold, then yes—Spirit *does* intervene.

We may not be able to stop every tragedy. We may not be able to rewrite the past or prevent every moment of suffering. But what we *can* do is *be the rowboat* for our fellow humans. We can be the love, the light, the evidence of something greater moving through us.

We can show up fully embodied. With empathy. With love. With open hearts and the willingness to be abundant—not just for ourselves, but so we can *give* from that overflow.

And when we show up in that way—when we show up with love—heaven really *is* a place on earth.

And yes, Spirit *is* there. Always.

Conclusion

When the opportunity to write this book first came up, I was ecstatic. This was the moment I had been waiting for since I was eleven years old, the moment I had dreamed of when I sat in my childhood bedroom, carefully writing a letter to random publishers, convinced that somehow my words would find their way into the world. I didn't know how publishing worked. I didn't know the ins and outs of getting a book deal. All I knew was that I wanted to write—that I had something to say, something to share. And that desire has never left me.

But I never could have imagined just how much life would unfold in the six months I spent writing this book. When I signed the contract and sat down to begin, I thought I knew what the process would look like. My sun sign is in Virgo, and I had imagined structured writing days, where I'd sit at my desk with a lit candle

CONCLUSION

or rent a secluded cabin by the water, typing away effortlessly as divine inspiration flowed through me. I had envisioned a creative process that felt almost cosmic—a beautiful, sacred experience filled with clarity and ease. But what actually happened was something entirely different.

Life didn't pause to give me the perfect conditions to write. It threw itself at me, full force. During these six months, I went on my first tour—an experience that stretched me in ways I hadn't expected. It was exhilarating, fulfilling, *exhausting*, and at times, overwhelming. I stood on stages, connected with people, shared messages from Spirit, and poured my energy into every event. And then, when the lights went down and the room emptied, I would return to my hotel room, open my laptop, and try to piece together the chapters of this book. Some nights, the words came easily. Others, I stared at the blinking cursor, willing the inspiration to return.

In the midst of it all, my dad was diagnosed with cancer. Suddenly, the book didn't feel as urgent as he did. There were phone calls, doctor updates, and moments of helplessness where all I could do was sit with the uncertainty. Even a road trip to Alabama with my sister to be with him got thrown into the mix. I sat in the hospital waiting area typing out portions of this book, wondering if he would be alive to read it. And yet, even then, Spirit nudged me forward. I wrote through it, allowing my emotions to pour onto the page, allowing my grief, my love, my growth edges, and my hope to be woven into the very fabric of this book.

Friendships ended—ones I'd thought would last forever. They were the kind of endings that leave you questioning

CONCLUSION

things—questioning yourself, what you could have done differently, whether the love you poured into the relationship was ever truly seen. And at the same time, new friendships were forming, unexpected, soul-affirming connections that reminded me that endings aren't just losses; they are also beginnings.

My grandfather crossed over. I navigated old wounds rising to the surface in ways I hadn't anticipated. I grieved, not just for him, but for versions of myself I had outgrown, for the comfort of things I had once known but that no longer fit. And yet, through it all, I also found something else. I found my wholeness. I found my abundance—not in material things or external validation, but in the deep knowing that I was exactly where I was meant to be, even when it didn't feel that way.

This book remained my anchor, my constant. No matter where I was, no matter what was coming up for me, the words found me.

I wrote on airplanes, in my office, on the floor of my apartment, in hotel rooms between events, by the beach with the sound of waves in the background, in coffee shops filled with the hum of conversation and clinking cups. I wrote early in the morning before the world fully woke up, and I wrote late at night, when exhaustion sat heavily on my shoulders but inspiration refused to let me sleep. Some days, writing felt like breathing—effortless, natural. Other days, it felt like pulling myself through wet cement, struggling to translate the emotions in my heart into something that resembled a few words, much less a sentence.

And yet, I kept writing. Step by step. Letter by letter.

Because this wasn't just a journey of writing. It was a journey of letting go and *becoming*.

CONCLUSION

A journey of deepening my understanding of the world around me, of surrendering to the unknown, of peeling back layers to see myself more clearly than ever before. A journey of trusting Spirit completely—not just in the messages I deliver to others, but in my own path, in the unfolding of my own life.

There were moments of doubt, when I questioned whether I had the right words, whether I was saying what I truly wanted to say, and whether this book would resonate with anyone at all. But then, just as I started to spiral, Spirit would step in. Sometimes, it was through a message from a friend, a synchronicity too perfect to ignore, or a sudden wave of inspiration that felt like it had been whispered straight from the Universe.

This book taught *me* as much as I hope it will teach others. It reminded me that healing is never linear, that trust is a choice we make over and over again, and that sometimes the most profound transformations happen when we least expect them.

Writing this book was not just about sharing my experiences, my journey, my connection with Spirit. It was about opening myself up—fully, vulnerably, honestly. It was about letting go of the fear that I had to have all the answers, that I had to present myself as someone who had it all figured out. Because I don't. None of us does. And that's the beauty of it. I didn't have to be perfect on these pages, I just needed to be honest.

Ram Dass said, "We are all just walking each other home." And we are all doing just that: learning, growing, and expanding in ways we can't always see in the moment, which leads us to deeper connection with ourselves and each other. And if there's one thing I've learned through this process, it's that life is never going to wait for the perfect moment. The Universe isn't sitting around, waiting for us to feel *ready*. It moves, it shifts, and we have the choice to resist that expansion or expand with it.

And maybe that's the real lesson.

That no matter where we are in life, no matter what challenges arise, no matter how uncertain the road ahead may seem, we *are* being guided. Even in the moments that feel like chaos, even in the grief, even in the moments that shake us to our cores, there is something greater at play. Something that is allowing us to not only experience change, but to transform.

And that's the core of this book.

This isn't just a book about mediumship. It's a book about transformation—about the beauty of surrender, tapping into the deepest parts of ourselves and trusting in the power that is within us. It's about the power of love and how, when we are brave enough to open our hearts, miracles are not only possible, they are abundant.

What Spirit Has Taught Me

One of the biggest truths I've come to understand through my work is that we do not die. I understood this the day the pastor shared the never-ending-cable story with me. Our loved ones are not *gone*. They are simply existing in a different frequency, still loving us, still guiding us, still showing up in ways that, if we pay attention, are impossible to ignore.

I have given thousands of readings, and in each one, Spirit finds a way to bring forward messages of love, healing, and often, the exact words someone needed to hear in that moment. Through these experiences, I've learned that connection with Spirit is not reserved for mediums—it's something we all have access to. Spirit communicates with all of us, whether through signs, synchronicities, dreams, or those sudden waves of knowing we can't quite explain.

Yet so many people doubt their own abilities to connect. They brush off signs as coincidences, dismiss their intuition, and hesitate to believe in what they *feel* to be true. But here's what I know: If you open yourself up to the possibility, Spirit will show up for you. And once you start paying attention, you'll never look at the world the same way again.

Synchronicity: The Universe's Language

Synchronicity has been woven into every chapter of this book because it's been woven into every chapter of our lives. It's something I experience every single day.

When a song with a deeply personal meaning plays at the exact right moment, when a stranger says something that feels like it was meant just for you, when you think about someone and they suddenly call you—those aren't accidents. That's the Universe winking at you, letting you know you're supported, that you're on the right path.

I've experienced this time and time again. Like the morning I described early after my dear friend passed, when I put my music on shuffle and the first song that played was "Separate Ways (Worlds

Apart)" by Journey—the very song she always sang at karaoke. That wasn't a random occurrence. That was a hello. Or the time I was on the beach, feeling deep gratitude for connection, and the family next to me began playing "September," the song that had been mentioned by my client's father in Spirit earlier that day.

Synchronicity is a reminder that we are not alone. That we are being guided. That Spirit, our loved ones, and the Universe are always communicating with us—we just have to be willing to listen.

Opening the Heart, Opening to Life

A huge theme in this book—and in my own journey—has been the lesson of *opening the heart*. For so long, I believed I had to protect myself. That if I let people in, if I let myself be seen, I would be opening myself up to abandonment or hurt. And while, yes, vulnerability comes with risk, it also comes with profound connection.

Spirit has shown me that when we close off our hearts, we don't just protect ourselves from pain—we also block ourselves from *joy*, from *possibility*, from the incredible experiences life has in store for us. We block ourselves from love. And not just romantic love, but the deep, soul-nourishing love of friendship, community, connection to *self*.

Throughout this book, I've shared moments where I've had to take the leap—whether it was stepping onto a stage, trusting Spirit in a reading, or recognizing that if I had the courage to open myself to Spirit, then I also had the courage to open myself to love. Trusting Spirit isn't just about receiving messages—it's about trusting life itself. It's about knowing that, even when we don't have all the answers, we are still being guided.

The Lessons I Take with Me

As I look back on the process of writing this book, I realize that I didn't just *write* it—I *lived* it. I lived the lessons of surrender. Of trust. Of acknowledging my own wounding and fear and stepping into expansion anyway. I lived the reminders that life is never going to wait for us to be *ready*—it will constantly unfold for us, and it's for us to decide if we are going to keep up with the expanded version of who we are after we let go of who we were.

This book has been a journey—through love, grief, connection, and the undeniable presence of Spirit. And maybe that's the real message I want to leave you with:

You are never alone—love, guidance, and connection are always available to you. When you open yourself to the Spirit within you, you open yourself to transformation.

We do not die. Our energy is eternal.

Our loved ones are not gone.

And if you open yourself up to the possibility—if you quiet the noise, trust what you feel, and pay attention—you'll realize something profound. Not only have you healed. You have transformed.

You are worthy. You are whole.

And Spirit has been with you all along.

I love you, and I'm incredibly proud of you.

—Travis

Exercises

How to Connect

By now, you're probably more than a little curious about how to connect with Spirit, your Guides, or your loved ones who have crossed over—for *yourself*. And honestly? I *love* that. My dream is to live in a world where, one day, mediums like me aren't needed—because everyone has discovered their own way to connect, to trust, and to feel the presence of Spirit in their own lives. Now, I realize that might be a *terrible* business model, but it's the truth. Because this work was never meant to be exclusive to a select few. Connection with Spirit isn't something reserved for "gifted" people—it's available to *all* of us.

You *already* have the ability to connect. You always have. It's not about learning something new—it's about remembering. It's about tuning back in to what's already within you.

EXERCISES

Throughout my journey, I've explored countless exercises and practices that have helped me tap into the energy around me—the same energy that is woven through everything, accessible to all of us at any moment. Some techniques have come naturally, some have taken practice, and some have completely surprised me. But all of them have led me to a deeper relationship with Spirit and, more important, a deeper relationship with *myself*.

In this section of the book, I want to share those practices with *you*. My hope is that these exercises help you find your own sense of connection and alignment with universal energy—so that you no longer feel you need to look outside of yourself for answers but instead can trust what's been within you all along.

Spirit is already speaking to you. The signs are already there.

Now, let's help you learn how to listen.

Sitting in the Power

Sitting in the power is the cornerstone of mediumship, intuitive development, and spiritual connection. It's not about *doing*—it's about *being*. It's about strengthening your connection to your own soul and to the energy of the Spirit world, allowing yourself to expand into a state of presence, receptivity, and alignment. Think of it as plugging yourself into the universal power source—charging up your energy, deepening your awareness, and creating space for Spirit to step forward. I say this knowing that I respond very well to it, however, you may not love it, and that's okay.

When you consistently practice sitting in the power, you build a stronger, clearer connection to Spirit. You become a more open

EXERCISES

channel. You deepen your trust in your own intuition and learn to distinguish between your energy and the energy of Spirit.

Putting It into Practice

This is a practice—not something to force but to surrender into. The more you do it, the easier and more natural it becomes.

1. **Find a quiet space.** Choose a place where you won't be disturbed. You can sit on a chair with your feet flat on the ground or cross-legged on the floor. Keep your spine straight but relaxed. Close your eyes.

2. **Ground yourself.** Before you expand, you need to root. Imagine your feet growing roots deep into the earth, anchoring you. Feel the support beneath you. This keeps you stable while your awareness rises.

3. **Connect to your own power.** Shift your focus inward. Feel the energy of your own soul. Imagine a light glowing within your chest, in the center of your being. This light represents you—your power, your essence, your divine spark.

   With each breath, feel this light expand. Let it fill your body, moving through your arms, legs, and head. You are not creating power—you *are* power. This is about feeling the inherent energy within you.

4. **Expand your energy.** Allow this energy to move beyond you, like a radiant aura growing larger and larger. It expands outward, filling the room. You are blending with the infinite power of the Universe.

EXERCISES

5. **Open to Spirit.** Once you feel present in your own power, invite Spirit to step closer. This isn't about calling in specific people, it's simply about attuning to the Spirit world. Imagine your energy lifting, expanding, merging with the higher vibrations of Spirit.

    You might feel tingling, warmth, pressure, or even a presence. Or you might sense nothing at all—and that's okay. Just sit, breathe, and allow.

6. **Rest in the stillness.** This is the heart of the practice. No expectations. No pressure. Just be in the power, feel the connection, allow whatever comes next. Some days, it will feel strong. Other days, quiet. But each time you sit, you are strengthening your ability to hold and recognize Spirit's presence.

7. **Gently return.** When you're ready, bring your focus back to your body. Feel your feet on the ground. Wiggle your fingers and toes. Take a deep breath and thank Spirit for the connection.

How Long Should You Sit in the Power?

Start with five to ten minutes and build up to fifteen to thirty minutes as you become more comfortable. Some mediums sit for an hour, but consistency is more important than length. I find that twenty minutes is the sweet spot for me.

EXERCISES

Creating Your Life

I believe in your ability to create the life that you desire for yourself. I believe it because I did it. I am not special in the sense that the Universe plays favorites with me. (I wish.) I just decided one day that the way I was living my life was no longer serving me and something had to change. For me, I had to be in emotional shambles, on the brink of self-destruction, ready for the floor to swallow me whole, but it doesn't have to be that way for you. You can decide to transform your life right here, right now.

As I mentioned earlier, I once thought manifestation/*The Secret* was a bunch of BS, akin to a get-rich-quick scheme. My story back then was that the only way to live a life that felt fulfilling was to struggle. I'm not saying there won't be times where we have to put in some work. But intentional, aligned action feels much different from grinding away with no real sense of direction. I've done both, and I can tell you I much prefer the former.

For me, manifesting, or intentionally creating my life, has become less about the material stuff I receive and more about becoming the person who receives abundance and joy and can hold on to it. This has become a way for me to get to the essence of how I want to feel each day: to allow the Universe to show up and surprise me in ways I can't imagine for myself.

We were born to expand. Our own universe is still expanding. The process of expansion is never done, and with new expansion comes new desires. If you feel bad for wanting more than what you have, that's an old story that isn't serving you. Of course, being grateful for what we do have is important, but by no means does that mean that all of a sudden we stop wanting conditions to shift. If we're hungry, we eat. And when we eat, we feel grateful for the meals we have in front of us. But we know we will be hungry again. Our desires work the same way.

Manifestation and You

A manifestation exercise that has truly changed my life isn't just about visualizing what I want or making a wish list for the Universe—it's about practicing the feeling of what I desire before it even shows up. Because here's the truth: We don't actually want the thing itself—we want what we *think* that thing will make us feel. And when we tap into that feeling now, before the physical manifestation appears, we align ourselves with it in a way that allows it to come in faster and more easily and sometimes in ways we never expected.

I totally get it. We want the money. We want the dream homes, the thriving careers, the soul connections who make us laugh until our stomachs hurt. I want those things, too. And guess what? It's okay to want them! Where we get hung up is needing those things in order to be happy. Desire is powerful. It's what moves energy, what calls in new experiences, what helps us grow. But if we dig a little deeper, those things all represent something much more significant: They represent how we want to feel. *Security. Freedom. Love. Excitement. Peace. Expansion.*

And here's the kicker—when you practice feeling these emotions before the thing shows up, you start vibrating at the frequency of your desire. The Universe, which is always responding to your energy, will begin sending you signs, synchronicities, and opportunities that align with the frequency you're putting out. You're no longer *chasing* what you want—you're becoming a match for it. And when that happens, the physical manifestation has no choice but to find you.

Manifestation Exercise: Feeling Your Way to What You Desire

1. **Grab a journal or a piece of paper and make two columns.**

2. **In the first column, list the physical things you desire.** Be honest. Don't hold back. If you want the luxury home, the successful business, the relationship that feels like a rom-com, write it down. Own it. If you want more time freedom, money freedom, or just to feel happy, write it down. If you don't know what you want, start by figuring out what you don't want.

3. **In the second column, next to each item, write down the feeling that desire represents.** What does that thing *actually* give you on an energetic, soul level? Is it freedom? Safety? Passion? Joy? Confidence? Abundance? Peace? It's okay if emotions overlap. In fact, that overlap can provide a lot of insight as to what it is you are really wanting.

4. **Put it together in an intention statement.** When we set intentions, we send an energy out into the Universe that allows what we want to come to us through inspired action and receiving. Your intention statement needs to be written

in the present tense, as if it's already happening. Here's an example: *I am grateful for the abundance that flows to me freely from multiple sources. I feel deep gratitude knowing the Universe supports me, and I am living out my dreams by doing work that I love and that serves others. I feel freedom knowing that I always have the ability to choose my path forward in life.*

5. **Now, close your eyes and practice feeling that emotion in your body.** Imagine what it feels like to already *have* what you're asking for. Let that feeling settle into your system like it's already yours. How does your body respond? What shifts in your energy? Do not focus on the outcome but rather focus on the feeling. Most folks are so well practiced in stress and struggle, so practicing something else might feel weird at first. Keep showing up and prepare for miracles.

6. **Commit to practicing this feeling daily.** The more you sit in the energy of what you want, the more your body and mind will seek out the things that *feel* like that feeling. When we practice the feelings of peace, joy, abundance, and freedom intentionally, we tend to steer ourselves toward things that resonate with that energy.

7. **Watch for signs.** You can ask your Guides or loved ones for specific signs that you are in alignment with the path you desire, or you can ask them to surprise you. The Universe will show you in multiple ways that it's not only listening but delivering.

8. **Trust in divine timing.** Some manifestations are instant, some may take a bit. There's no set time limit; it all depends on how much resistance we have on our paths and

how willing we are to dive in and allow ourselves to let go of what's holding us back. Go easy and know that simply feeling better *is* evidence that you are on the right path.

9. **Be open to how it comes in.** And here's the final piece—the Universe may deliver it in a way that looks different from what you imagined, but trust that whatever shows up is an exact match for the energy you've been embodying.

The goal isn't just to *get* the thing you're thinking about. The intention is to start living in the energy of what you desire *right now* because that's what brings you what is in your heart. From there, the Universe will bring you experiences that help you define further what you truly want. So if you experience something that you thought you wanted but it doesn't feel the way you hoped, that's okay! You can always change the energy around your desire. And the best part? When you shift your energy, the Universe *always* responds.

No matter the exercises you do, they have to feel good to you. The Universe responds to how we feel, not how we pretend we feel. Faking it until you make it won't cut it. The Universe rewards our authenticity, not our bullshit. The thing that gets you amped up the most about connecting to your loved ones in Spirit or manifesting your desires will also attract them the most easily.

We are vibrational beings, and when we radiate from our places of power, the Universe responds in kind. Please remember that this is a journey and an unfolding. The practice that works for

EXERCISES

you today may not resonate for you next week, and that is okay. Since starting my journey, I have had many rituals. The ones I've described above just so happen to be the ones I always fall back on when I need something tried and true. Please experiment with your own. That's the fun part!

Happy manifesting!

Acknowledgments

I have not been on this journey alone—not even close. Every step, every breakthrough, every moment of doubt and triumph has been shaped by the incredible souls I've met along the way. There are people who have lifted me up, people who have challenged me, and people who have shown me love in ways I never expected. And for each and every one of them, I am deeply, eternally grateful.

Every person who has crossed my path—whether for a fleeting moment or a lifetime—has given me something precious. A lesson, a piece of wisdom, a reminder of who I am and what I'm here to do. Some have been my greatest supporters, some my greatest teachers, and some, without even realizing it, have shifted the entire course of my life. I carry those gifts with me every single day.

So to those who have walked beside me, believed in me, and even to those who unknowingly shaped me from a distance—thank you. This journey wouldn't have been the same without you.

ACKNOWLEDGMENTS

Thank you to Spirit, for allowing me to do this work of receiving the gift of connection and transformation and sharing it with others.

Thank you to every person who bought this book, who follows me on social media, who comes to my shows, who's booked a reading with me. Serving you is an honor of a lifetime, and I do not take it for granted. Thank you.

Mom—I am so grateful to be your son. You are such a beautiful example of the power that love has to transform, and I would choose you lifetime after lifetime to be my mom. Thank you for being who you are. I love you.

Dad—Thank you for teaching me the power of doing something that you are passionate about and for teaching me what it means to have a strong work ethic.

Sister—You were my first friend and have been a constant in my life. You've been there through every version of me—and I'm so grateful for you.

My nephews—I am so incredibly proud to be your uncle. Your laughter and joy remind me what is important in life.

Pam and Randy—Thank you for being the best bonus parents/stepparents anyone could ask for and for helping both my parents start their new chapters in life.

My bonus family: Ben, Will, Siy, Zach, Ed, Matthew, Hunter, Ryan, Kenny, Benjamin—You are more than friends; you're my

ACKNOWLEDGMENTS

family. Thank you for your constant support and for believing in me. "Because I knew you / I have been changed for good." —*Wicked*

Lo—There aren't enough words. There just aren't. I love you.

Melissa—Everyone needs a friend who sees your vision and tells you to go for it. Thank you for being that friend.

Len E. & Jeff D.—The best publicists. Thank you for seeing what I'm capable of, even when I don't always see it for myself right away.

MaryAnn DiMarco—Thank you for your guidance, wisdom, and support. You're the best!

David P.—Thank you for believing in this book and my vision for it. I'm so grateful our paths crossed.

Spiegel & Grau—I'm deeply, deeply grateful for you all and your support with this book. Thank you for taking a chance on me.

Eleven-year-old Travis—Look, buddy, we did it! I love you, and I'm incredibly proud of us.

References

Brown, Brené. *Daring Greatly: How the Courage to Be Vulnerable Transforms the Way We Live, Love, Parent, and Lead.* Gotham Books, 2012.

DiMarco, MaryAnn. *Medium Mentor: 10 Powerful Techniques to Awaken Divine Guidance for Yourself and Others.* New World Library, 2022.

DuFrene, Troy. "Two Boats and a Helicopter: Thoughts on Stress Management." *Psychology Today*, May 4, 2009. www.psychologytoday.com/us/blog/fumbling-for-change/200905/two-boats-and-a-helicopter-thoughts-on-stress-management.

Hicks, Esther, and Jerry Hicks. *Ask and It Is Given: Learning to Manifest Your Desires.* Hay House, Inc., 2004.

Swart, Tara. *The Source: The Secrets of the Universe, the Science of the Brain.* HarperOne, 2019.

About the Author

TRAVIS HOLP is a sought-after medium and spiritual guide known for his remarkable ability to deliver profound insights filled with hope, healing, and joy that resonate deeply with audiences worldwide. Born in Dayton, Ohio, he now resides in Tacoma, Washington.